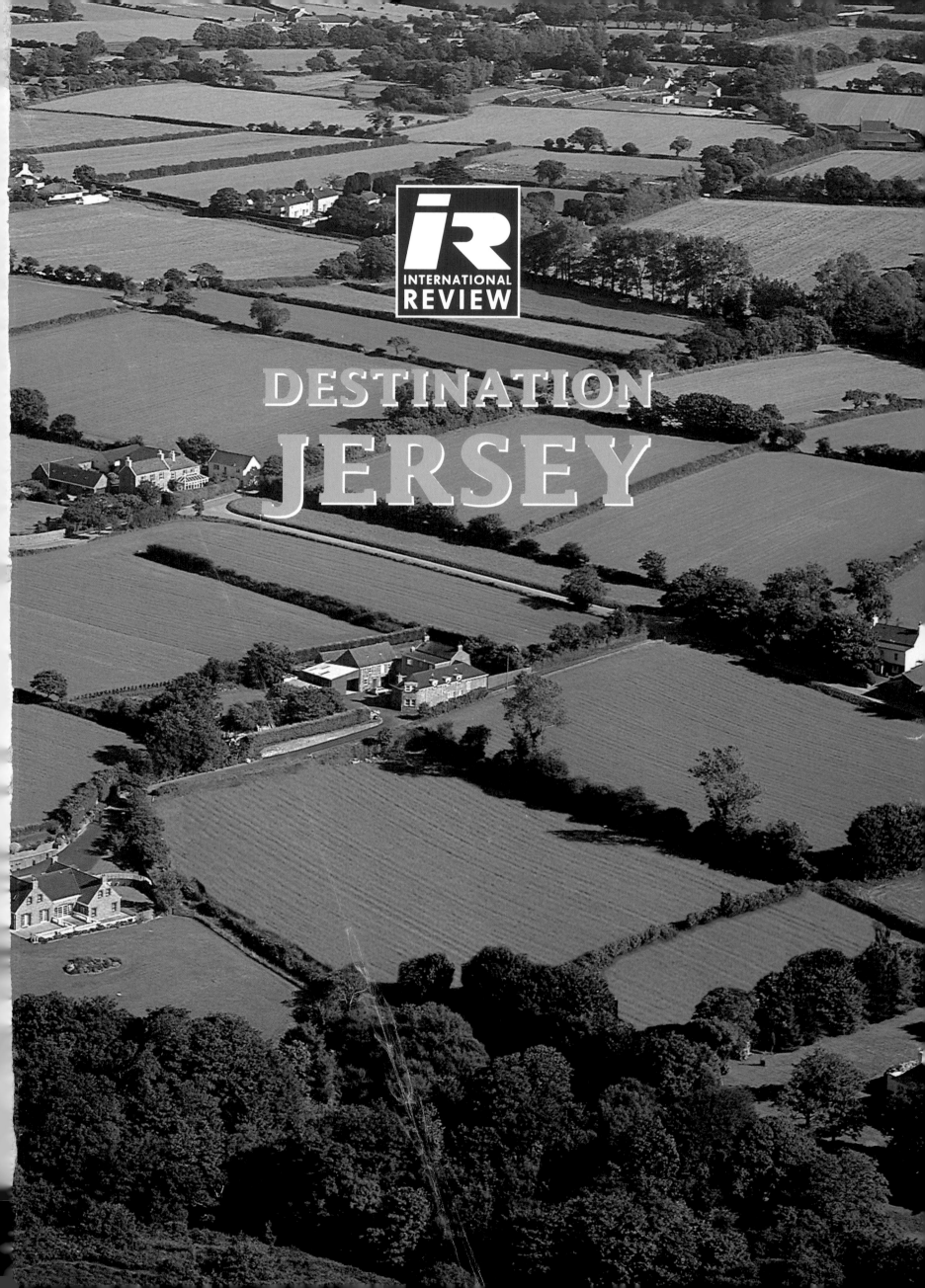

DESTINATION
JERSEY

iR INTERNATIONAL REVIEW

MICHAEL J. PHILLIPS
Publisher & Editor-in-Chief

Terry Brisco . . . . Executive Editor
Patrick Keuleers . . . . Production Director
Patrick Lambregts. . . . . Production Director
Benoit Roland . . . . Photographic Director
Daniel Philippe . . . . Director Aerial Photography
James Graham. . . . . Marketing Director
Sylvia Phillips . . . . Translation Director
Kris Van Beek . . . . Production Supervisor
David Phillips. . . . . Public Relations Director
Peter Janssens . . . . Art Director
Walter Remeysen . . . . Graphic Designer
Jurgen Toune. . . . . Graphic Designer
Herman Stoffels . . . . Design Editor
Dirk Van de Sande . . . . Text Editor
Debbie Phillips . . . . Editorial Director
Antoon Lauryssens . . . . Image Editor
Marc Aerts. . . . . Graphics Editor
Nille Tilley . . . . Graphics Editor

Publisher   Review Publishing Company Ltd, United Kingdom

Printer   Brepols Graphic Industries, Turnhout, Belgium

Production   Review Publishing Company Ltd, Antwerp, Belgium

Lithography   De Schutter Group, Antwerp, Belgium

Photography   Professional Colour Services Ltd, St. Helier Jersey, Clive Coutanche,
Michael Bewley (pg 100-101), Stuart McAlister, James Morgan,
Richard Gibson, Liam Du Feu, Jersey Evening Post

We would like to thank the following for their helpful collaboration:
Phil Austin, Hans Bärlocher, James Baudains, Tim Bettany, Peter Body, Diana Booth,
Robert Christensen, Michael Day, Sue De Gruchy, Environmental Services,
Trevor Falle, Doug Ford, Mike Freeman, David Greenwood, Steve Hunt,
Jersey Arts Centre, Jersey Finance, Jersey Heritage Trust, Beth Lloyd, Val Nelson,
Robert Parker, Colin Powell OBE, Dr. Edward Sallis, David Tipping

DISTRIBUTION

Great Britain   Review Publishing Company Ltd
Unit 1, Leigh Green Industrial Estate,
Appledore Road, Tenterden, Kent TN30 7DF, UK
Fax: 44-1580-765 056

Belgium   Altera Diffusion
Rue Emile Féron 168, B-1060 Brussels, Belgium
Tel: 32-2-543 06 00 Fax: 32-2-543 06 09

Luxembourg   Librairie Ernster, rue de Fosse, 27, L-1536 Luxembourg
Tel: 352-225077-1 Fax: 352-225073

The Netherlands   Betapress bv, Burg. Krollaan 14, NL-5129 PT Gilze
Tel: 31-161-45 78 00 Fax: 31-161-45 2771

All other countries   Review Publishing Company Ltd
Rue François Libert 12, B-1410 Waterloo, Belgium
Tel: 32-2-353 18 80 Fax: 32-2-687 29 42

ISBN 0-9535447-4-5

CONTENTS

www.internationalreview.com
e-mail: international.review@skynet.be

Editorial

As an international publisher of some 35 years' standing, I am delighted to have this opportunity to turn the spotlight on Jersey. Though small, this island enjoys a worldwide reputation for its offshore banking and finance sector, a success story that has gone from strength to strength for some four decades with the promise of further growth in the years to come.

Yet I have also been impressed by many other aspects. Not least the sheer beauty of the scenery to be found around every corner and cove. At times peaceful and pastoral, both land- and seascapes here can also be awe-inspiringly rugged and powerful – a poignant reminder of the way the elements have shaped this island and its proud people over the centuries. That others also feel the same attraction to those natural features is self-evident, given the thousands who regularly choose Jersey as their destination for rejuvenating short-breaks and carefree summer holidays.

Efforts to diversify the economy appear to be paying dividends. A number of innovative firms in the technology and distribution sectors have made the island their base, creating valuable new jobs and enhancing the profile of Jersey abroad. For this is an island which cherishes its rich past – such as its age-old traditions, fine cuisine and colourful festivals – while looking to the future with confidence.

Wherever I have stayed in Jersey to conduct my research for this publication, I have been received with warmth and openness, for which I thank everyone sincerely. This is an inherently friendly and self-supportive community, yet one which is patently delighted to welcome visitors from all over the globe. In this book we have done our very best to offer a panoramic overview of this fascinating island. So it now simply remains for me to wish you happy reading!

Michael J. Phillips
Publisher

Introduction

Lying in the Bay of Mont St. Michel, the Bailiwick of Jersey comprises the largest of the Channel Islands (45 square miles or 116 sq. km) and the two small uninhabited reefs known as the Ecréhous and the Minquiers. Jersey lies some 100 miles (161 km) south of mainland Britain and 14 miles east (23 km) of the French coast.

Jersey is unique in many ways. The island has its own fiscal and legal system, backed up by island law courts. Income tax is a flat rate of 20%. Islanders also have their own passports and car registration plates. Notes and coins issued here are in sterling, but have their own original design.

In common with the other Channel Islands, Jersey benefits from a mild climate, with summer temperatures averaging 20°C and little frost in the winter. This is because of the prevailing wind from the south-west and the Gulf Stream, which together ensure the climate is warmer than one would expect at a latitude of 49°N.

The island annually enjoys an average of 2,000 hours of sunshine, more than anywhere else in the British Isles, delighting both holidaymakers and farmers. Also exceptional are the island's tides, with a range between high and low water of as much as 40 feet (12 m).

Around a third of the island's population, which totals some 87,000, lives in the capital and financial centre of St. Helier. The island is made up of 12 parishes, namely Grouville, St. Brelade, St. Clement, St. Helier, St. John, St. Lawrence, St. Martin, St. Mary, St. Ouen, St. Peter, St. Saviour and Trinity. They have their origins in the 11th-century ecclesiastical make-up of Jersey, a structure that has become the basis for its civil administration. Each parish is headed by a Constable (Connétable), who represents local government and has his own elected police force known as 'honoraries', complementing the paid local force.

Jersey is part of the British Isles but not part of the United Kingdom. Nor is it a member of the European Union. Ties with the British mainland are with the heirs to the Dukes of Normandy, the English Crown, not with Parliament. Following King John's loss of his French possessions in 1204, the islanders remained loyal to their sovereign. As a result, they were granted certain rights – confirmed and extended by later English kings – which led to the island becoming self-governing. Jersey's parliament, called the States (from the French 'états'), is one of the world's most ancient legislatures. As the island has never sent representatives to sit at Westminster, Acts of Parliament only apply to Jersey if it is specifically agreed that they should. The Royal Court is one of the oldest law courts in the world, dating back to the Middle Ages.

The States of Jersey are currently made up of the 53 members and the Crown appointees. The voting members are the Deputies, who represent districts, the Constables who represent the parishes, and Senators who are elected on a whole-island mandate.

States meetings are chaired by the Bailiff, who is appointed by the Crown and acts as the Speaker. He is also the president of the Royal Court. While the Bailiff is allowed to speak in the Assembly, in order to ensure an orderly debate he has no voting powers other than the casting vote – which by tradition is used to maintain the status quo. When absent, his position is taken by the Deputy Bailiff, who is also appointed by the Crown.

Other Crown appointees are the Lieutenant-Governor, who serves for five years, and the Dean, who is head of the Anglican Church in the island. The Law Officers – the Attorney General and the Solicitor General – can speak in the chamber to clarify points of law, but they have no votes.

The island's economy is dominated by the banking and finance industry, supported by an active tourist sector. A fairly unique combination that looks set to prosper for many years to come.

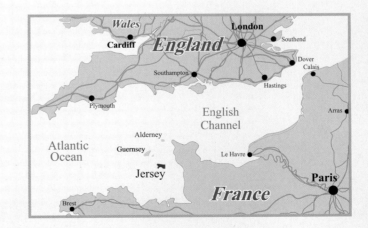

History

The Charter granted to the island in October 1663 by King Charles II, confirming the immunities and privileges of the islanders

Raiders from the sea

Mention the word Jersey and immediately many from outside the island think of the state of New Jersey in the United States. The word also calls to mind a knitted jumper, a type of fine woollen or silk cloth, a variety of early potato and a breed of cow known for its creamy milk, high yield and appealing eyes. Few people associate the name with the Channel Island of Jersey. Yet for such a small place, Jersey has one of the longest records of human activity in the world.

Over a quarter of a million years ago, bands of nomadic hunters used a cave in what is now St. Brelade as a base for hunting mammoth. The bones and tools they left behind can be seen at the Jersey Museum. This wandering lifestyle ended some 8,000 years ago, when Jersey became an island and the first farmers made their appearance. These Neolithic settlers lived in settled communities and left their mark on the island landscape in the form of ritual burial sites and standing stones known as dolmens and menhirs – the most dramatic of which is the burial site at La Hougue Bie. Around a third of all the stone axes found in the island had been brought in from what is now Brittany or southern England.

There was no bloody conquest. The island was simply absorbed into the Roman world and was known as Andium and later Angia. In the 5th and 6th centuries, following the collapse of the Roman Empire, the Channel Islands were on the migration route of the British settlers who moved out of Britain and into Brittany. This is often known as the Age of the Saints, when itinerant holy men such as Saint Sampson, Brelade and Helier were all active in the area.

The island finally became known as Jersey when

Sir Walter Raleigh, Governor of Jersey from 1600 to 1603

the Vikings arrived in the area in the 9th century. Their presence was formally recognised by a French king in 911, when he granted the Norsemen's leader Rollo the land around the mouth of the River Seine – a region now known as Normandy.

The Channel Islands had been politically linked with Brittany until 933, when Rollo's son, William Longsword, seized the Cotentin peninsula and the islands and added them to his domain.

In 1066 William, the seventh Duke of Normandy, invaded England and defeated King Harold at Hastings. Jersey's link with the English Crown was established. The island remained part of the Duchy of Normandy until 1204, when King Philippe Auguste of France conquered the duchy from his cousin King John of England. The islanders remained loyal to John and Jersey was recognised as a personal possession of the English king.

From 1204 onwards the islands ceased to be a peaceful backwater and became a frontier post on the edge of a war zone – a potential flashpoint in international relations between France and England. Jersey's royal fortress of Mont Orgueil was built at this time to emphasise the English king's power. During the Hundred Years' War, the island was attacked many times and was even occupied by the French for a couple of years in the early 1380s. Perhaps the most famous incidents involved the great French military leader Bertrand du Guesclin, who led his raid in 1373, and the Spanish adventurer Pero Niño in 1406.

Because of their strategic importance to the Eng-

The turbulent Middle Ages

Battle of Jersey, January 6th 1781

Sir Anthony Paulet, Governor of Jersey from 1590 to 1600

lish Crown, the islands were able to negotiate a number of benefits for themselves from successive kings. When England was divided by the civil war known as the Wars of the Roses, the French occupied Jersey for seven years between 1461 and 1468. The Yorkist Admiral, Sir Richard Harliston succeeded in retaking the island for Edward IV. During the 16th century the islanders adopted the Calvinist form of the new Protestant religion and life became rather austere. French Huguenot refugees came to settle in the island to escape the Wars of Religion which were raging in their own country. The increasing use of gunpowder on the battlefield meant that fortifications had to be adapted and new ones built. The first of the new

British warships off the coast of St. Helier in 1740

buildings was St. Aubin's Fort, erected in the 1540s on the islet guarding the haven of St. Aubin. At the same time the local militia, first mentioned in 1337, was reorganised on a parish basis and each company had to have two cannon that were usually housed in the church. In St. Lawrence a blocked doorway used by the militia cannon can still be seen today in the west wall of the church, while the only remaining militia cannon from this period can be seen at the bottom of Beaumont Hill. In the 1590s, after it was realised that St. Aubin's Fort was too small, a new fortress was built on the site of the old abbey church on the two small islets near St. Helier. While he was Jersey's Governor, Sir Walter Raleigh named this new castle after his queen.

Jersey's main export at this time was woollen goods. In the early 17th century the production of knitwear reached such a scale that it threatened the island's ability to produce its own food. The States (local government) intervened and passed laws regulating who was allowed to knit and when they could do it. Any man found knitting in the company of women who were not members of his own family could be imprisoned. Jersey stockings were highly prized in France, resulting in the development of a thriving smuggling trade.

During the 1640s England was divided by Civil War – King against Parliament. The hostilities spread into Scotland and Ireland and eventually to Jersey. While the islanders' sympathy lay with Parliament,

the de Carteret family held Jersey for the King. In 1646 the Prince of Wales and his brother the Duke of York sought refuge in the island and they returned for a second time in 1649, following the execution of their father, King Charles I. The Viscount, Edouard Hamptonne, proclaimed the young prince King Charles II in the Royal Square.

A Parliamentarian invasion force finally captured the island in December 1651. The English Civil War was over. Enemies of the state were imprisoned in the old castle at Mont Orgueil. The most radical of these were Colonel John Lilburne, the leader of the Levellers, and General Robert Overton, the leader of the Fifth Monarchists. Five years later, leading figures from the Parliamentary years were imprisoned in the island because their politics had become too extreme and amongst the new batch of prisoners were five of the men who had signed the king's death warrant.

Following the restoration of the monarchy in 1660, Charles II rewarded the States of Jersey for their loyalty to him during the Civil War. His present, a ceremonial mace, can still be seen in the States

Departure of Queen Victoria from St. Helier in 1846

Halkett Place in the 1840s

Royal Square in the 1830s

Shipbuilding in Gorey in the 19th century

Race meeting at Grouville Common in the 1850s

building today. The king also granted George Carteret a parcel of land between the Hudson and Delaware Rivers in the American Colonies: this became known as New Jersey. On his death in 1680, his widow Lady Carteret sold the state for £3,400 to a group of men led by the English Quaker William Penn.

This was not the only link the island had with the Americas. As early as the 1530s it was said that six islanders accompanied the Breton explorer Jacques Cartier on the expedition that explored the mouth of the St. Lawrence River in Canada. By the end of the 16th century, islanders were returning with cargoes of salt cod from the Grand Banks of Newfoundland. Thus began a thriving industry which would last over three hundred years.

Boats would leave the island in late February or early March following a service in St. Brelade church – the Communion de Terre Neuviers – and the men did not return until late September when the season was over. By the end of the 18th century, Jerseymen were more involved in the carrying trade than in the actual fishing. Jersey merchants built up their business empires in Newfoundland, Nova Scotia and Gaspé. The greatest of these companies was set up by Charles Robin in the late 18th century. Other companies, such as the Le Boutilliers Nicolles, Janvrins and Fruings, were all active in the Gaspé region – which in Jerriais, the islanders' native tongue, was simply referred to as La Côte or the Coast. The cod trade was very import to the island economy. In the 1770s, over 2,000 men and boys were engaged in it – which works out at around 10% of the entire civilian population of the time travelling thousands of miles in search of fish every summer.

The cod trade reduced the efficiency of the island militia, since many of its officers and men were missing for long periods. This was certainly bad news in the 18th century, when political tension was growing again between the British and the French, intent on expanding their trading empires worldwide. Frequent clashes occurred between these nations. As a result, because of its geographical position, Jersey found itself almost permanently on a state of heightened alert.

During periods of hostilities, Jersey seamen took advantage of their proximity to the main trade routes and acquired letters of marque which allowed them to become privateers. This allowed them to attack enemy shipping without being branded pirates. Channel Island privateers were held in high regard by the English government, as they freed up Royal Navy ships to serve in other parts of the world. The French were particularly keen to try to prevent Channel Island privateers taking to the high seas and therefore targeted the islands.

During the period of the American Wars of Independence, there were two attempted invasions of Jersey. In 1779, the Prince de Nassau tried to force a landing in St. Ouen's Bay and was beaten off by the garrison and the militia. Two years later a force led by the French gentleman adventurer Baron de Rullecourt succeeded in capturing St. Helier in a daring dawn raid. The acting commanding officer of the British garrison in the island, 24-year-old Major Francis Peirson, ignored orders to surrender issued by the Lieutenant-Governor, Moise Corbet, who was held prisoner by the French. Peirson marched his troops and the militia into St. Helier. A short battle in the Royal Square resulted in a British victory, but during the fighting both Peirson and de Rullecourt were killed. Another battle took place at Platte Rocque, in which the French

Queen Street at the turn of the 20th century

Passenger aircraft were still using West Park beach as a runway in 1936

St. Aubin in 1847

rearguard was defeated. Despite being 3,000 miles away from the main theatre of war, these two battles were essentially part of the American Wars of Independence.

The peace that followed the wars was short-lived, for in 1789 the French Revolution broke out and thousands of refugees fled to the island. When war broke out in 1793, Jersey was the base for a very successful counter-revolutionary spy network, La Correspondence, which was headed by the Prince de Bouillon – a title held by the Jerseyman Philippe d'Auvergne. One of the most successful agents was Armand de Chateaubriand, the cousin of the great French poet. In the novel 'Quatre-vingt-treize', Victor Hugo modelled his character Gelembre on this agent. The islanders once more took to the seas and applied for letters of marque, but the French were more successful this time and by the end of 1795 over 40 Jersey vessels and their crews had been captured by the French.

Jersey changed forever after the Revolutionary and

the Napoleonic Wars, because of the rapid growth in the number of English-speakers there – especially at the English-speaking garrison and the Royal Naval squadron also stationed in the island. After 1815, many retired British army and naval officers moved to Jersey to enjoy life on their half-pay pensions. This trend, combined with the large number of English-speaking labourers who flocked to the island to work on the Esplanade and harbour projects between the 1820s and 1840s, resulted in Jersey gradually adopting English as its main language. The final nail in the 'French cultural coffin' was driven home in the 1870s, when the States decided that the language of instruction in island schools should be English.

In the five decades following the Battle of Waterloo, Jersey developed as one of Britain's major shipbuilding centres. Island shipyards launched more than 900 vessels, the largest being over 1,000 tons. The introduction of steam engines and iron ships meant that Jersey shipbuilders could no

Tourist transport in 1926

longer compete in the market and so the industry disappeared. At the same time, the island developed as a major centre for the spring oyster fisheries, employing over 3,000 people on the boats and in the shore gangs. New piers were built at Gorey, Rozel, Bonne Nuit and La Rocque to accommodate the influx of English fishermen. This industry disappeared in the 1860s, due to over-fishing.

As the island maritime industries disappeared, farmers benefited from two agricultural developments – the Jersey cow and the Jersey Royal potato. In 1789 the States

banned the importation of live cattle into the island and the breed we now know as the Jersey was gradually developed in the first half of the 19th century, until its milking qualities were recognised throughout the world and a steady export business was built up. While the development of the cattle breed resulted from selective breeding programmes, the appearance of the variety of new potato known as the Jersey Royal was a total fluke. Hugh de la Haye grew the first Royals on his farm in 1880 and within ten years over 65,000 tons of new potatoes were being shipped out to the English market.

The Great War affected the island in the same way it affected most parts of Britain and France: men joined up and went to the trenches to fight at the Front. However, the Second World War was totally different, for this time the war came to Jersey. On 1 July 1940 thousands of German troops occupied the island and remained there for almost five years. Some 8,000 islanders managed to evacuate Jersey or join the British forces before the arrival of the Germans; a further 1,200 were deported to internment camps in Germany, and more than 300 were sent to prisons and concentration camps in mainland Europe. The Channel Islands were finally freed on 9 May 1945 and Liberation Day has been celebrated as a public holiday ever since.

Jersey as we now know it results very much from a decision taken by the States in October 1962: their repeal of the 18th-century law against usury created the conditions for today's finance industry to flourish. The finance industry is now the island's largest employer and by far the largest contributor to the States' coffers.

Jersey was occupied by the Germans from 1940 to 1945

The Jersey Railway in 1870

JERSEY TODAY

Residents are never far from the beach

Jersey's geographic position somewhat resembles its economic and political status. It is on the edge of the European Union and close to the UK, but is a part of neither. This separation has resulted in a community used to making its own way in the world and achieving success by living on its own wits.

Loyal to the UK, but with a distinct French flavour, Jersey has managed to retain its own character despite the onset of globalisation and the spectacular growth in the financial services industry. The island even has its own language, Jersey French, still officially the mother tongue of sev-eral hundred people in the country parishes.

Islanders claim to be fiercely loyal to the UK and its sovereign, but would object equally fiercely if the UK government tried to inter-fere in Jersey's affairs. This is a community familiar with enjoying the best of both worlds. Few people can explain in detail the unique constitutional relation-ship between the UK and the Channel Islands, and there are outstand-ing questions over this relationship which have never been tested in the courts. Jersey, along with Guernsey and the Isle of Man, are Crown Dependencies. As every

A clean environment

schoolchild on the island knows, Jersey's link to the UK is through the monarch – a title taken in 1066 by the Duke of Normandy, whose possessions already included the Channel Islands.

Jersey has never had representation in the UK par-liament, and the parliament cannot legislate for the Channel Islands without their consent. How-ever the UK government is said to have the ulti-

A stable currency

14

The States in session

mate responsibility for 'the good government' of the islands – although what this exactly means has never been spelt out.

In a typically British way, this unwritten and slightly uncertain constitutional relationship has worked well over the centuries. The islanders have enjoyed their independence, while the UK has been happy to look after Jersey's foreign affairs and defence, and generally protect its interests.

The UK welcomes the growth of Jersey as an offshore finance centre, which has brought the island considerable wealth and produced income per capita considerably in excess of the 'mother country'. This development came about because Jersey has essentially been a tax haven for centuries and immune from UK taxation. In days gone by, the English monarch could have imposed the same levy on his possessions as he did in England.

But successive kings and queens have rewarded the islanders for their loyalty by exempting them from UK taxes and duties. Now it is virtually inconceivable that the UK could impose taxes on the island or interfere with its system of taxation, without the consent of the islanders.

Keeping up with ever-changing international financial standards is proving very challenging for a small jurisdiction such as Jersey. Yet the island has devoted considerable resources to ensuring that it remains in the forefront of these developments – without giving a competitive edge to other finance centres, which may be slower or more reluctant to adopt the same standards.

A more subtle change springing from the success of the finance industry can be seen in the community's growing 'sophistication'. Not all islanders are wealthy, but many regularly dine out in fine restaurants, drive luxury cars, travel frequently and generally enjoy a good lifestyle. Those with a penchant for culture are well catered for, through museums, music and theatre venues, and the 100 year-old Opera House. Likewise, sport and leisure facilities are of a high standard and certainly much better than one would expect in a relatively small community.

Yet there are other sources of revenue. Tourism has contributed significantly to the island's wealth for nearly two centuries. Today it is the second biggest industry, bringing in revenue of more than £250 million a year. In the past two decades, however, the sector has contracted significantly, as the traditional British tourist looking for a cheap summer beach holiday has gone further afield. There are now, for instance, only around 15,000 hotel beds available, compared to 25,000 in the early 1990s.

The island has tried to adapt to the changing market. Jersey is now promoted much more as a short-break destination, or a resort for people who do not want to spend all of their time on the beach and who are more interested in good food, an attractive environment and a unique culture and history.

Agriculture is now valued not so much for its economic contribution as for the role it plays in preserving an attractive countryside and maintaining the island's rural culture. Jersey was largely a rural community up to the German Occupation during World War Two, and although the way islanders make a living has changed dramatically, many of them come from traditional local families or still choose to live a mainly rural lifestyle.

Most families in Jersey now make their living from banking, investment management, trust and company administration, accountancy, the law or other related activities such as information technology or telecommunications. That said, these sectors have required additional manpower with skills that are not readily available in the island. This influx has resulted in the island's biggest problem, too much success – which is mainly why Jersey's population has increased from around 69,000 in 1971 to just over 87,000 today.

Now the island is split roughly into two camps. Those who want to stop immigration because of overcrowding and the impact this has on the environment; and those who want to allow some

Tomorrow's leaders

immigration because of the need to protect economic growth. Virtually no-one believes that large-scale immigration should be allowed.

Limiting immigration presents a major challenge for the island. Because of its role as an offshore finance centre, Jersey needs more and more personnel simply to ensure that the island complies with new laws and regulations which are being introduced at a tremendous rate. An ageing population also means that there is growing demand for nursing and medical staff.

There is also a demand for more government employees, because although growth in government spending is limited, even a jurisdiction as small as Jersey has to deal with increasingly complex international issues. For example, although Jersey is not a member of the European Union, it tries to match EU standards in areas that are relevant, such as consumer protection and the environment.

The increase in administrative complexity has also convinced the island that it needs to update its machinery of government. The current governmental system, with no political parties and a

High-quality health care is readily available

JERSEY TODAY

An infinite variety of restaurants

First-class sporting facilities

parliament made up of 53 independent members, produces a very democratic system. Attempts to reform the government and produce a leaner system with a stronger executive is gradually bearing fruit.

While Jersey obviously faces many difficulties, history shows that its people have adapted to changing circumstances and have always managed to find a niche where they could make a living. They have managed to achieve economic success, while also preserving a traditional island way of life and protecting a unique environment.

They have also maintained a caring society with few major social problems and very little crime compared to neighbouring countries. A mugging would be a rare front-page story in the local newspaper. Much of the credit for this must be given to Jersey's 13 police forces – a professional uniformed island-wide police service and an elected

Lush green countryside

An outstanding education system

Popular entertainers regularly visit Jersey

unpaid, voluntary police force in each of the 12 parishes. The honorary police provide true community policing, with officers known as Centeniers and Vingteniers elected by the parish. Little goes on in any parish, particularly the less-populated rural ones, that the honorary police do not know about.

There is no unemployment benefit in Jersey, so anyone who is struggling financially because of unemployment (also a rarity here) has to apply to their parish for assistance. Their plight will usually be examined by the Constable, the official head of each parish and someone often referred to as 'the father of the parish'. The lack of widespread unemployment undoubtedly stems from the success of the finance industry, which also provides the tax revenue needed to pay for the high level of government services in Jersey.

All of the schools, whether private or state-run, are of a very high standard, and examination results are consistently higher than the UK average. Medical services are also first-rate and hospital treatment is free for residents, although there are private facilities for those who want private care. Social security contributions, which amount to just over 5% of an employee's salary, pay for a range of benefits – all of them more generous than those provided in the UK, especially state pensions.

Looking to the future, the island understands it faces many challenges. But if success is measured in the number of people who want to live and work in Jersey, then this island can be called a tremendous success story.

Rich in culture

A patriotic people

Island of flowers

Retailers offer variety and value

A world-class financial centre

The international currency

By Phil Austin,
Chief Executive,
Jersey Finance Limited

The historical origins of the Jersey finance industry are deep-rooted and the island's association with banking and low taxation can be traced through the centuries. The largest of the Channel Islands, close to the mainland of northern France but inextricably linked to the Crown of England for hundreds of years, Jersey has frequently found a niche in which it has excelled and as a result successfully sold its services worldwide.

From knitting in the 16/17th centuries to shipbuilding and cod fishing in the 19th, the island's major industries have always flourished. As one sector declined, new ones developed. In the 20th century, agriculture and tourism became vital industries – joined since the 1960's by financial services. Over the last two decades, the finance industry has evolved into the island's dominant revenue provider – thanks in great measure to Jersey's independent fiscal position.

We have to turn back the pages of the history books to find the beginnings of that independence. From the 10th century, the island was ruled by the Duchy of Normandy, before becoming involuntarily linked with England through the Norman Conquest of 1066. The first date often quoted as relevant to today's finance industry is 1204, when King John of England relinquished his hold on lands on the French mainland. That year, Jersey's main landowners chose to remain loyal to the throne of England and King John.

This decision had far-reaching consequences, with the island remaining loyal to the British Crown ever since. Yet through various charters, granted by the English Crown, Jersey has maintained its independence from the rule of England. Thus Jersey has its own Parliament, the States of Jersey, which is responsible for all its domestic laws. In 2004 the island will celebrate a constitutional relationship with London that dates back 800 years. It is this relationship that ensures the island authorities have complete autonomy over all domestic affairs, including fiscal policy and taxation.

The island has been a low-tax area for centuries. To secure its loyalty, successive English monarchs granted Jersey charters that exempted it from English tax. According to the charter in 1468, written during the reign of Edward IV, the king "... have of our special grace granted to the said inhabitants that they, their heirs and successors shall be as free... from the payment of all kinds of dues, customs, subsidies... and other duties to us or our successors in the Kingdom of England, as fully as the said inhabitants of Jersey or their predecessors have ever been."

Close International Asset Management

Personal Financial Services for the Offshore investor

English-speaking, politically stable location where familiar banking names were present. Jersey has maintained this traditional appeal, while widening the appeal of the jurisdiction to overseas investors, including many foreign expatriate customers. The island offers them legitimate fiscal benefits and provides investment products which are truly portable: that is an important consideration for career professionals who regularly move around the world.

1979 was an important year for the finance industry's expansion. The UK government removed the exchange controls that had extended to the Sterling area as a whole, including Jersey, and this move opened Jersey up to more and more international business. The buoyant international trading and investment climate in the 1980s also resulted in a tremendous growth in private wealth – which led to an increase in demand for private banking facilities, investment management and other financial services (particularly from residents in countries with unstable political and economic conditions).

Another significant fiscal date was September 1940, shortly after the start of the German Occupation. The island authorities found it necessary to increase the rate of income tax from 2.5% to 20%, a rate that has remained unchanged ever since. From this historical backdrop it is easy to appreciate that Jersey's increasing popularity as a low-tax area in the second half of the 20th century arose naturally from its status. It did not need higher taxes to maintain a successful economy.

The first bank on Jersey was established in 1797. But the modern industry, as we now know it, can be traced back to December 1961 when the Merchant Bank, then known as M Samuel & Co., became the first City of London institution of its kind to join the handful of traditional high street banks in the island. They began offering a more sophisticated type of financial product.

Figures illustrate the sector's dramatic growth, especially in the second half of the 20th century. In 1903 bank deposits in Jersey totalled £2 million, increasing modestly to £19m by 1939 and £40m by 1960. By then, however, the world was changing and, with the granting of independence to numerous former British Colonies, many UK expatriates sought a safer refuge for their funds. Fiscally and politically stable Jersey, although not a part of the UK, was a Crown Dependency and proved attractive to them. Yet there was a small, historical barrier to Jersey playing host to financial institutions keen to manage this money. A provision in a code dating back two centuries, to 1771, remained in force, limiting interest to a maximum

of 5%. The island's government eventually repealed this provision in 1962. Within 10 years, 25 banks and other deposit-taking institutions had established a presence in Jersey and total deposits had increased to some £500m.

Today Jersey is home to just over 60 banks, holding deposits totalling £135 billion, with some two-thirds of that amount in foreign currencies. Even in recent times, between 1999 and the present, deposits have continued to rise consistently – underlining the jurisdiction's long-standing appeal to investors. The island's investment managers look after more than 23,000 clients and the amount of funds under management, though difficult to quantify exactly, is in the region of £107 billion. Without doubt, these figures highlight the extent to which our finance industry has been a remarkable, modern-day success story for the island.

Foreign investors are attracted by the financial framework. As noted, Jersey has complete fiscal autonomy in setting its tax rates. The island has neither capital gains taxes, estate or inheritance duties, nor value-added, sales or other taxes applying to fees or charges for professional services. Other advantages – besides the island's economic and political stability for many decades – include being in the British time zone, proximity to the English mainland and the City professionals' familiarity with the Channel Islands.

Building on the private client and trust work in the 1960s, the 1970s saw the island's banks introduce services for expatriates – particularly British expatriates, who were attracted to an

AIB Bank

Jersey's finance industry today has grown beyond all original expectations, offering incredible breadth and depth in its services. In the space of just a few decades, this sector has changed not just the face of the island's economy but that of the island itself. The finance industry comprises many thousands of people working in a broad range of disciplines. It also provides services for clients, private and corporate, from over 200 countries.

Another important factor for the sector, in addition to its constitutional relationship with the UK, is the island's position and status within the European Union. Jersey's standing within the EU is defined by Protocol 3 of the Treaty of Accession of the United Kingdom to the European Community. The island is not a separate member state or an associate member of the EU. Jersey complies with EU directives on trade in industrial and agricultural products, but is not bound by directives or regulations in other areas, such as European Monetary Union, taxation or financial services. There is sometimes discussion in the media and elsewhere about the island needing to follow measures recommended by the EU. But because Jersey sits outside the EU, it is not obligated to follow its advice or directives.

However, the island authorities and the finance industry are keen to cooperate with the many international initiatives that emerge from time to time, including those emanating from the EU. As Jersey is not part of the EU, it has to examine and assess the impact of any measures on its own economy. Just as the EU has the interests of its

Aberdeen Private Wealth Management

The financial world never sleeps

own members to consider, the island must also look after its best economic interests. Therefore agreement on proposals, particularly where they affect Jersey's fiscal position, will not always be reached immediately. Negotiations are often required to discuss the impact and to work out the final detail. Our primary concern, whenever new measures are implemented, is for there to be an international level playing field.

The financial services industry is an increasingly competitive market and our competitors are global. They include EU finance centres such as Luxembourg and Dublin. Naturally, the island has to take great care when it agrees to regulations, insisting that other centres also adopt the same measures. However, all jurisdictions share the same aim, which is improved standards of regulation and legislation to help protect the legitimate investor and to support global efforts to catch money launderers, fraudsters and terrorists. Many of the new measures are designed to help in the global fight to crack down on terrorist funding. Jersey is fully supportive and already has comprehensive anti-money laundering legislation and Orders which will help us freeze assets should any terrorist funding be detected. In fact the island has maintained a leading-edge approach to new legislation. In 2001, we saw the introduction of the Financial Services (Jersey) Law, which extended the requirement of registration to trust and company service providers and imposed stricter regula-

tion on their operation. The tightening of the rules in the trust and company area followed on from earlier legislation designed to regulate investment business in Jersey. Prior to that, the island was one of the first to embrace the need for more stringent anti-money laundering legislation through the introduction of the Proceeds of Crime Law.

The finance industry in Jersey is also supportive of the call for more transparency and openness in financial services both offshore and onshore. These developments are good news for financial services clients worldwide.

The long-established nature of Jersey's finance industry is a primary reason for its remarkable breadth and diversity. The range of skilled professionals working in banking – and in the related fields of investment, funds, trust and company work, legal and accounting services

Dexia Private Bank

– has played a major role in Jersey's more recent success. This world-class skills base provides the springboard for a host of innovative products and services, and has helped the industry to develop successful niche business.

I can illustrate this diversity with two simple examples. The use of a trust for the protection of assets has always been one of the prime tools in the island's financial services industry. However, trust business is evolving. In the 1960s and 1970s, the focus was primarily on estate planning for wealthy individuals. Today trust business is far more diverse. Trust structures, for example, are used to support the establishment of employee share-ownership schemes and other vehicles designed to help international businesses manage their staff-incentive and employee-share schemes on a global basis. As a result, Jersey has become a prominent centre for employee-benefits business. Many companies from the FTSE 100 have found that the legislative environment and the skills available in Jersey are ideal for administering their global employee-benefit plans.

Over the last decade, Jersey has increasingly been used as the jurisdiction of choice in the European zone for establishing securitisation vehicles; this significant development shows no sign of abating. The number of special purpose vehicles set up to meet the needs of institutional business in this regard grows every year. Private equity schemes

Standard Chartered Grindlays

and commercial property transactions structured in Jersey in appropriate special purpose vehicles prove popular with some of the world's leading banking groups.

Also central to the island's success is the attitude and approach of the Jersey Financial Services Commission, the independent regulatory body. It has implemented regulations which have earned warm praise from influential overseas organisations, among them the Financial Stability Forum, the Financial Action Task Force and the US Department of State. At the same time, the Commission has maintained a flexible approach when considering specific structures, in order to offer the industry a bespoke service.

The Commission has built up a considerable store of expertise in special purpose investment vehicles and is able to draw on this knowledge when considering applications. The island continues to witness growth in the number of institutions based in leading centres – such as London, Paris and New York – using Jersey structures to set up private equity and venture capital funds and to run captive insurance companies.

In an introduction to the island's financial services industry, I cannot hope to cover all the diverse aspects of the business. Personal banking services for wealthy individuals and overseas investors generally remain the backbone of the industry, together with the specialist services for corporate clients noted above. In addition, the island is able to promote itself as "a one-stop shop" for quality solutions for accountancy, tax and audit; corporate and trust law; trust and company administration; investment management advice and dealing; international pensions and life assurance; mutual fund products and fund administration; treasury operations; global custody; and all classes of insurance and reinsurance, including captive.

Jersey has been pre-eminent in the offshore finance industry for 40 years. Consequently, as a mature offshore jurisdiction, it is able to offer a wealth of experience in handling the needs of the offshore investor across a broad spectrum of financial services. Private client and institutional business sit side by side, bonded by a common denominator: a commitment to delivering high-quality services in a properly regulated environment.

Clerical Medical Investment Group

Bank of Scotland International

Private banking pioneer

Hill Samuel, a respected name in Jersey banking for over 40 years

Hill Samuel Private Bank and Trust Company, which forms part of the Lloyds TSB Group of companies, has been operating in Jersey for over 40 years. It was the first merchant bank and non-high street clearing bank to establish an operation in the Channel Islands and can justly claim to have been the forerunner of today's flourishing financial services industry. It was also the first Channel Island bank to target non-resident investors.

Hill Samuel came to Jersey following an invitation from the States of Jersey to establish a presence in the island. The bank opened its doors for business in December 1961, and is proud to have been the catalyst for what is today one of the world's most reputable offshore finance centres.

Today it offers traditional private banking values to discerning clients. Services available include a dedicated relationship manager, regular client meetings and comprehensive investment information. Clients are also provided a wide range of banking, investment and trust solutions, designed to achieve their financial objectives.

The origins of Hill Samuel are rich and colourful, beginning in 1833 when Marcus Samuel senior founded a small firm near the Tower of London to import goods from the Far East. Business grew steadily, with an increasing range of goods imported and exported across the world.

In the late 19th century, Marcus Samuel junior made his first moves into the relatively young oil industry. As this aspect of his business grew, he named it Shell Transport & Trading Company, named after the popular sea shells his father had been importing from the Orient. Shell Oil was born. He was knighted in 1898 and, as Lord Mayor of

London in 1903, laid the foundation stone of the present Baltic Exchange.

By the 1920s, M. Samuel & Co. had become recognised as a major merchant bank, prospering with an extensive acceptance credit business and strong associations with overseas banking houses. Hill Samuel & Co. Limited was formed in 1965, following the merger of M. Samuel & Co. with Philip Hill, Higginson, Erlanders Limited, creating one of the largest merchant banks in the City of London. By this time Hill Samuel was already firmly established in Jersey, providing offshore banking services.

In 1987 the Hill Samuel Group was acquired by TSB and in 1995 became part of the merged Lloyds TSB Group. Today, more than 40 years since it arrived in Jersey, Hill Samuel is proud of the flexible, efficient and innovative service it provides to personal and corporate clients in Jersey and overseas.

Serving private and corporate clients worldwide

Jersey head office of ABN•AMRO Bank, a leader in international private banking

Prestigious private banking

With its full branch status in the island for almost three decades, ABN•AMRO Bank N.V., Jersey is situated in the heart of St. Helier's business community. The company recently moved into imposing new offices, reflecting its commitment to increase efficiency and to expand its extensive range of services and products.

One of the world's top banking groups, ABN•AMRO has over 3,500 branches located in 70 countries. Whilst the group has its headquarters in the Netherlands, it enjoys a deserved reputation for being a strong and universal bank with an international focus.

Thanks to its position within one of the group's three strategic business units, Private Clients & Asset Management, the Jersey branch is able to provide leading banking, investment management and estate planning services. These are increasingly important to private clients seeking to preserve and enhance their wealth in an often complex and volatile world. The Jersey Centre also can tap into the professional expertise and international opportunities afforded within the group.

The Jersey branch is already capitalising on the attractive and modern facilities in its new offices on Castle Street. Staff now benefit from a specially designed working environment, not to mention a state-of-the-art computer suite, a large dealing room and the latest communications technology. The Jersey Centre plays an integral role in the group's offshore and trust businesses, and has grown alongside the island's developing finance industry. Moreover, the new premises and recent raising of the firm's profile dovetail neatly with the group's strategy of concentrating on private clients and all their requirements – locally, nationally and internationally. In addition to this, extensive

treasury and corporate banking services are offered to local intermediaries and large international companies.

Offering a broad range of sophisticated banking and investment services, the branch is committed to providing exemplary service. In private banking, this begins with an in-depth assessment of a client's individual circumstances, needs, priorities and aims. Each client has a dedicated private banker, uniquely positioned to offer advice and to recommend appropriate and sometimes tailor-made products. Regular contact with clients, as well as continual performance measurement, ensure that best-of-breed solutions are implemented – and also updated as personal requirements and global markets evolve.

Services are mainly targeted at high net-worth individuals. In addition to offering highly personalised banking for private clients, the Jersey Centre provides traditional banking, investment advisory services, discretionary portfolio management, as well as international estate planning and trust services.

A notable feature is the Treasury team, one of the largest in the Channel Islands. It provides money-market deposit rates and foreign exchange quotes in all major currencies, plus an extensive range of structured treasury products. An active dealing team also allows for clients' treasury and corporate banking activities to be initiated and executed offshore.

More dynamic services are ideal for growing wealth. Under investment management, clients can actively develop a personal investment strategy, supported by their private banker, or let professional portfolio managers do so on a discretionary basis. As for estate planning, the branch assists with structuring the ownership of worldwide assets, optimising tax situations, and setting up offshore companies and/or trusts.

Committed to placing clients at the heart of its service, ABN•AMRO Jersey adds value throughout its banking and investment services.

Tailor-made private banking

Dexia BIL, the result of a successful three-way merger in 1995 between major banks in France, Belgium and Luxembourg, has become a leading player in Europe's financial sector. Today the Group boasts total assets in excess of EUR 350 billion, a global staff of more than 25,000 and one of the best credit ratings in the world. It is also an acknowledged leader in public and project finance in the United States and several European countries.

Much of the bank's success stems from a strategic growth policy founded on cross-border alliances and acquisitions. Proud of its European organisation and vocation, Dexia is active in 12 European countries and listed on the Brussels, Paris and Luxembourg stock exchanges.

Dexia Private Bank Jersey Limited was founded in 1995 and is today well-established in its home island. It has a diversified financial base, thanks to a comprehensive range of private banking products and services. Right from the start, this thriving subsidiary has handled offshore business for a broad spectrum of international clients. Many of these clients – who hail from more than 40 countries – find their way to the Bank through introductions from professional and financial advisers. Core banking services available include deposits, loans, overdrafts, multi-currency credit cards, foreign exchange trading, and cheque books.

Personal contact with clients underpins the success of this Jersey-based bank. The highly qualified staff, who are fluent in all major languages, pride themselves on their ability to offer a tailor-made and confidential service. This service is based on open dialogue and the assignment to customers of personal advisers. In addition to working closely with the client at the outset of a relationship, so as to define objectives, these advisers remain in regular contact, reviewing and fine-tuning client profiles and investment goals whenever necessary. Advisers also liaise with managers and financial experts throughout the Group or beyond, to ensure a customer's portfolio is running to plan.

Under the broad umbrella of investment management services, asset management forms a key service at Dexia Jersey. A strong team of professionals seeks to achieve performance for all clients, whilst controlling risk. As ever, the Bank pursues these goals by skilfully combining traditional values – discretion, security and confidentiality – with innovation, helped by new technologies and developments in financial markets. Tailored investment is based on the approach of local access to global markets, as well as original research, advisory services, a range of financial instruments and careful risk control.

With modern offices in St. Helier's central banking district, Dexia is focused on enhancing its brand awareness in Jersey and beyond. The roll-out of

Dexia's offices in the heart of the banking district of St. Helier

Dexia's integrity, trusted by clients worldwide

upgraded Internet products, such as Dexia Plus, is also sure to bring in new business, as is the recent availability of guaranteed products from a new team in Luxembourg. The growing demand for private banking throughout the world and a legitimate requirement for offshore services to wealthy private clients provide further opportunities for Dexia in Jersey.

Teamwork, the key to success

Group Executive

of share classes covering Global Equities & Bonds, with regional equity funds giving exposure to North America, Europe and Asia Pacific.

These core competences are the foundation of the Group's rapidly expanding "optimised" private client and institutional Global Wealth Management Service. The service aims to deliver consistent absolute returns with low volatility and a reduced correlation to bond and equity markets through the blending of the Group's multi-manager "best of breed" approach to traditional and alternative asset management. The Global Wealth Management Service leverages and expands upon the Group's depth of investment experience and products and is regulated in Jersey by the Financial Services Commission and in the UK by the Financial Services Authority.

In a continuing period of negative equity performance, private clients, pension fund managers and fiduciary professionals are looking for an alternative solution to manage their diminishing wealth.

LEADING-EDGE ASSET MANAGEMENT

Liberty Ermitage Group is one of Europe's largest offshore fund management operations, and delivers sophisticated, innovative and leading-edge investment solutions.

The Group prides itself in its ability to think differently. It challenges traditional investment conventions using a rigorous and dynamic fund selection and risk management process, which embraces both in-depth macro analysis and fund manager evaluation.

Established in 1996 by Ron Mitchell, the Group's Chief Executive Officer, Liberty Ermitage is the offshore arm of the Liberty Group, South Africa's third-largest life insurance company and itself a member of the Standard Bank Group. Combined assets under management exceed $30 billion and aggregate market capitalisation is $5 billion.

Liberty Ermitage itself boasts assets under management exceeding $2.3 billion, run by a team of 16 leading and highly experienced investment professionals. It is headquartered in Jersey with acti-

vities in London, Luxembourg and Bermuda and an overall headcount of 55.

Hedge funds are a core business, spanning conservative hedge funds of funds, "white-labelling" for institutions who do not have the Group's research capability, the sponsoring of single manager hedge funds and specialist fund administration in Luxembourg. Liberty Ermitage has one of the largest research and investment engines in the industry and launched Jersey's first hedge fund in 1997.

The Group's highly conservative hedge fund of funds, Asset Selection and Alpha, are designed to deliver cash-like returns in extreme market conditions and multiples of cash over three years or more in a more constructive environment. Additionally, the funds are expected to out-perform the Salomon World Government Bond index over a similar time frame, with a considerably lower risk profile. The Group's long-short equity fund of funds – North America, Europe, Emerging Markets & Japan – seek to capture a high percentage of the performance in rising markets, whilst avoiding losses in falling markets. In this way the Group seeks to outperform market indices and provide investors with superior risk-adjusted returns.

Hedge funds are not the whole story. Liberty Ermitage launched Jersey's first Money Market Fund in 1996 which has been awarded Micropal's prestigious 5-star ranking and a Standard & Poors AAAm rating. Additionally, the Group has a traditional fund of funds umbrella, comprising a range

Head Office, Liberty Ermitage Group

They are turning to seasoned asset managers, who are able to deliver consistent, persistent and superior risk-adjusted returns. The Group typically delivers optimised wealth management solutions through bespoke discretionary mandates, which result from detailed discussions with the investor as to their investment experience, desired risk profile and both tactical and strategic investment goals.

Noted for its rigorous and proven research processes, covering alternative and traditional funds, Liberty Ermitage makes investment decisions which are heavily focussed on qualitative rather than quantitative insights. This bias, validated by its superior risk-adjusted and consistent investment performance over the years, offers clients a greater ability to preserve and enhance wealth in all market conditions. For the investor seeking leading edge investment products and services, Liberty Ermitage is the answer.

Jersey office of Gartmore Fund Managers International Limited

The retail fund management sector flourished for 20 years, but it changed substantially due to a combination of tax changes in the UK and the effects of the 1995 UCITS Directive (which gave rise to the EU-based fund administration centres of Dublin and Luxembourg). The UK retail business became gradually less important and the industry became increasingly institutional and international.

So why has Gartmore, a retail fund administrator with 25,000 investors and £2 billion under administration, survived? "Quite simply because we are experienced, flexible and think international – just like Jersey," says Martin Dryden, the company's managing director. Its flagship offshore fund, Gartmore Capital Strategy Fund Limited (CapStrat), launched in the summer of 1984, was almost certainly the world's first true umbrella fund. It brought together a number of ideas, such as single pricing, free switching, daily dealing and non-certificated shares within a corporate structure plus an independent board of directors. The concept was revolutionary at the time and has often been copied since. Today, CapStrat has investors from over 110 countries, particularly from continental Europe.

Serving clients worldwide

Jersey is a small island and the booming financial services industry has led to labour shortages in some sectors. Yet Gartmore, with around 35 staff based in St. Helier, has found little difficulty in recruiting or retaining staff. "Jersey, whether it be tourism, agriculture or financial services, operates in niche markets," says Mark Hill, the firm's operations director. "We like Jersey because it has a client service culture and a multilingual workforce. The island's diverse financial services industry, coupled with its emphasis on training, has allowed us to build a highly effective and scalable fund administration operation. We compare vary favourably with the competition."

Outsourcing has been a significant trend for many financial services companies over the past few years. Gartmore has not followed the trend and outsourced to Dublin or Luxembourg. "We are able to provide a fuller service than virtually any other external service provider," adds Hill. "We can also be more flexible and responsive. With outsourced partners, it costs every time you want to change something. In Europe you can get away with a standardised product offering, but internationally flexibility is everything."

Gartmore's senior management team has been together since before the 1987 stock market crash. The experience it gained riding out that turbulence has proved invaluable in the difficult financial markets of recent years. The company recently underwent a major internal restructuring, to address the growth of its German business. In order to bring about a big departmental reorganisation, the client service staff went away on a team-building exercise, which involved walking across broken glass. "It was a difficult weekend for all of us," recalls Dryden, "but we learned a lot about ourselves and about each other. After that, nothing is too difficult!"

Top-flight fund administration

Directors John Dimond, Nigel Parker and Managing Director Martin Dryden

Gartmore Fund Managers International Limited, part of the Gartmore Group, celebrated 25 years in Jersey in September 2000. The anniversary is significant, underlining that the company was actively involved in the development of Jersey's fund management industry from the start.

The industry was launched when UK fund managers set up subsidiaries in Jersey, to take advantage of the relatively low rates of capital gains tax compared to income tax in the 1970s.

Gartmore's first fund, the Gartmore Gilt Fund (Jersey) Ltd, was promoted almost exclusively to the clients of UK independent financial advisers.

Parish of
ST. HELIER

St. Helier, looking south-east

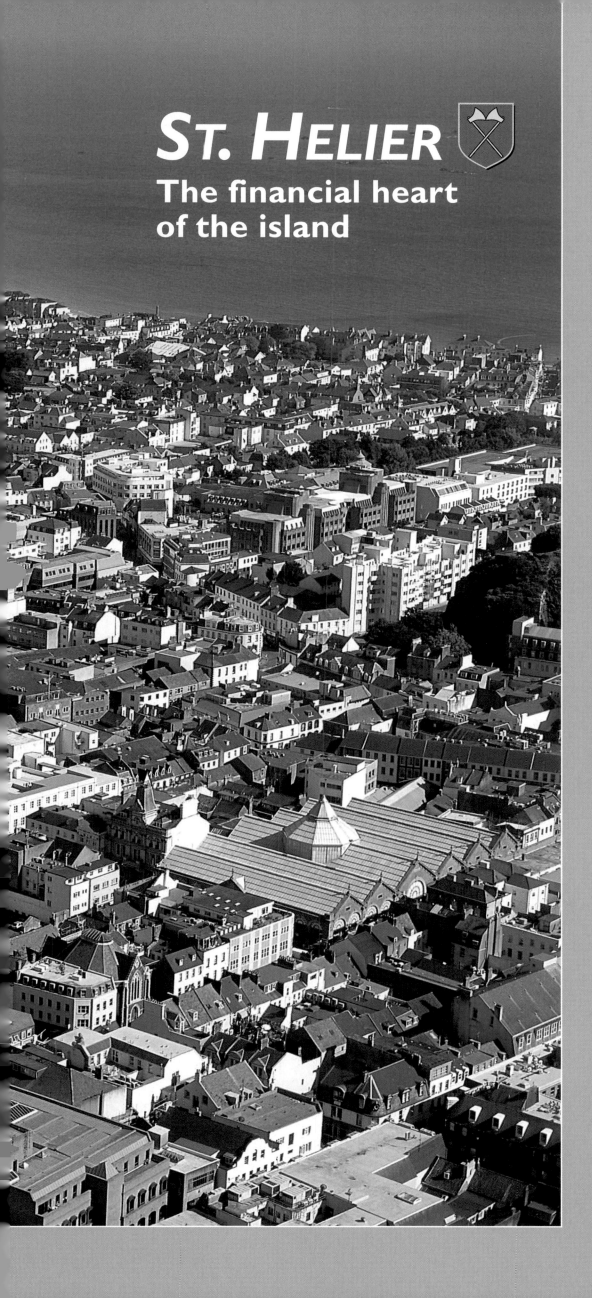

ST. HELIER

The financial heart of the island

Today the bustling capital of Jersey, St. Helier was fairly small until relatively recently. The town's population swelled in the 18th and 19th centuries, thanks to the influx of French refugees and then British soldiers. St. Helier parish, which shares borders with four other parishes and includes some land reclaimed from the sea, is now home to around a third of the island's population.

The town derives its name from a hermit who brought Christianity to Jersey in 540 AD. According to legend he lived for 15 years on a rocky islet in St. Aubin's Bay, next to the site of what is now Elizabeth Castle, before meeting a nasty end at the hands of seafaring marauders. The parish crest – two crossed axes on a blue background – still refers to this important episode in the history of the town and the island.

St. Helier is the first port of call for people arriving in the island by ferry from the UK and France. Just a short distance inland, they enter the busy and charming old heart of the town. This is the island's main shopping centre, centred around King Street and Queen Street. The granite-paved streets are pedestrian-friendly and packed with stores catering to every taste and pocket – with the added attraction of lower prices than on the UK mainland. The town also offers a wide range of cafes, inns and restaurants, popular with residents and visitors alike.

Central Market sells fresh Jersey produce of every kind. Opened in 1882, this colourful place features granite walls, a cast-iron roof and dome and a unique ornamental fountain. Nearby Beresford Market is smaller and specialises in locally caught fish, including crab and lobster.

Many banks and financial institutions are headquartered in the town. They are now the lifeblood of the island's thriving economy – in terms of both revenue and employment.

The island's government is situated in Royal Square. A single building accommodates the States Assembly – one of the oldest parliaments in the Commonwealth, the Royal Court and other government offices. The building houses a number of historical paintings, including a copy of The Death of Major Peirson – honouring the valiant soldier who helped to fight off French invaders in 1781 and who died nearby. St. Helier has several other important administrative bodies, such as the passport and immigration office, located in the harbour area.

Elizabeth Castle, stretched across two islets, is one of the island's most impressive buildings. Constructed in the late 16th century, it stands as the town's sea sentinel and can be reached on foot by a causeway at low tide or by amphibious vehicle at other times. The grey granite structure was designed to replace the medieval castle at Gorey, ultimately considered too vulnerable to artillery fire. Sir Walter Raleigh, the famous British adventurer and court favourite, was governor of the island when the new castle was completed and named it after his queen, Elizabeth I. The building, later extended on several occasions, acted as a temporary refuge for the future Charles II during the English Civil War and was occupied by the Germans during World War Two. One of its islet bases also hosted an abbey, which was destroyed several centuries ago.

Liberation Square

Liberation Square

To bolster defences, the authorities built another stronghold atop the hill overlooking the port. Fort Regent, a Napoleonic-era building, boasts outstanding views across St. Helier and St. Aubin as well as the east of the island. Completed in 1814, the huge white-domed fort has been converted into a multipurpose centre for sports and entertainment. It is also used for conferences, exhibitions and shows throughout the year.

The main religious building in St. Helier stands opposite Royal Square. Dating back to the 11th century, the parish church has served at times as an arsenal, storage area and even an asylum. The building has been frequently modified down the centuries, resulting in a mix of architectural styles. Not far from here, on a brief missionary visit in 1787, Methodist preacher John Wesley delivered one of his stirring sermons. Another great public speaker, French man of letters Victor Hugo, lived on the town's outskirts from 1852 to 1855, in the parish of St. Clement. He regularly met up with other French exiles at the Rocher des Proscrits, a large beach rock also nearby, but this time in St. Saviour's.

Sculptures and statues are dotted in and around the town. Measurements to all the island's milestones are taken from the statue of King George II, perched on a plinth in the Royal Square. A statue of Queen Victoria, a regular visitor to the island, stands at the eastern end of Victoria Avenue in Victoria Park. More recent sculptures include Les Jongleurs at Snow Hill and one of dolphins – centrepiece of the water maze at Les Jardins de la Mer. In 2001, to mark the Year of the Jersey Cow, a bronze sculpture of a group of Jersey cows was unveiled in Wests Centre. Liberation Square has a magnificent statue of a group of seven people hoisting the Union Jack – erected to commemorate the 50th anniversary of the island's liberation. Cultural enthusiasts will find plenty of interest in St. Helier, especially the handful of museums clustered close to the harbour. The Jersey Museum,

The Liberation Monument

Liberation Day is observed on 9 May every year

opened in 1992, calls on modern technology and dramatic displays to tell the story of the island, its traditions and industries. Close by, on the New North Quay, stand the Maritime Museum, the Occupation Tapestry Gallery and the Ariadne steam clock. The Maritime Museum delights visitors with its hands-on attractions and has been widely acclaimed. Alongside, in a purpose-built gallery, the Occupation Tapestry offers a moving insight into life in Jersey during one of its darkest periods and contains panels made by volunteers from all twelve parishes.

The arts are well provided for in the island's capital. It is home to the Opera House, recently restored to its former glory, the Jersey Arts Centre and St. James – a former church converted into a venue for performing arts. These centres promote a range of entertainment throughout the year, as well as hosting exhibitions and theatre tours. As for art galleries, the Town Hall owns a major collection of paintings, including 18 atmospheric watercolours of Jersey done by John Le Capelain (1812-48), while Jersey Museum stages regular exhibitions. The Jersey Eisteddfod, an annual arts festival, has played a regular part in the island's life for nearly a century, showcasing a wealth of local artistic and cultural talent through concerts, plays, as well as art and craft exhibitions.

More spontaneous entertainment is common during the summer months, when the town's streets are filled with street entertainers and musicians. In the weeks leading up to Christmas, late-night shopping and street entertainment are very much associated with the Fete du Noue.

Several spectacular events take place in and around the area. St. Aubin's Bay provides a dramatic setting for the Battle of Britain air display, held every September, featuring many different aircraft and traditionally concluding with the world-famous Red Arrows. A carnival atmosphere always accompanies the annual Battle of Flowers, renowned for its floral floats and bands. The first battle honoured the coronation of King Edward VII and Queen Alexandra in 1902 and is today a major tourist attraction.

Open spaces, parks and gardens abound. Parade Gardens, situated west of the town centre, incorporate lawns, flower borders and a children's play area, as well as an imposing monument to Lieutenant-Governor Sir George Don. The annual remembrance day service takes place at the Ceno-

taph, bordering this park. Peoples Park, on the western fringes, provides a popular open area. Across the road lies Victoria Park, site of the parish's recently erected Millennium Cross. Just above here is Westmount, a steep hill overlooking St. Aubin's Bay and on which the public gallows stood until the early 19th century. Its entrance marked with a dolmen, St. Andrew's Park at First Tower acts as another green lung in what is now a residential district.

The waterfront, developed on land reclaimed from St. Aubin's Bay, has extended St. Helier to the south. This area, where residential and leisure facilities are under development, now includes a new harbour terminal and marina.

Swimmers can indulge in their favourite pastime at the local beaches or at West Park, where the bathing pool retains the seawater at low tide. The same is true of the carefully restored pool and recreational facilities at Havre des Pas, on the east side of town. Shipbuilding once flourished in this area, later developed into a Victorian seaside resort replete with hotels and guesthouses.

St. Helier's status as the island's commercial, residential and financial heart seems assured in the 21st century. Especially now that this parish, so completely dominated by the town, is inexorably extending its boundaries seawards in order to pursue its burgeoning development.

The Cenotaph on The Parade

Liberation Day

The statue of General Sir George Don, Lieutenant-Governor of Jersey 1806-14, in the Parade Gardens

31

Wealth Creation

By Trevor Falle,
Managing Director,
Ashburton (Jersey) Ltd.

Jersey, a leading player on the world's financial stage

Most investors actually have the same aspirations. To preserve capital, minimise risk and volatility and achieve consistent results. The scale of the investment industry globally means that investment management services are still available in the main global financial centres but are also accessible almost anywhere, including on the Internet and by electronic mail.

However, while the characteristics of successful portfolio management may be the same for most investors, the circumstances of each investor are personal to them. So a key issue when selecting a portfolio manager is to establish a direct relationship on the basis of trust.

Careful analysis of investors' needs will determine attitude to risk and their expectations for a return on their investment. Investment was always intended to be for the long term, but the industry has a case to answer in this regard. Fortunately, the public has become wary of advertised performance figures and the fact that '...past performance truly is no guide to the future.' A portfolio of funds or asset types will be composed by the competent investment manager to suit each investor's specific needs and will be adapted over time to reflect the status of the client in relation to their life cycle. Tax, of course, is a secondary consideration but an essential one and requires a further layer of expertise and advice.

All of these skills are available in Jersey and have been for many years. It is difficult to put a precise number on the volume of assets that are actually managed from Jersey. However, to reflect the growth in our investment industry generally over the last 10 years, it is worth noting that the value of collective investment schemes under management in Jersey increased from £13 billion in December 1991 to £103 billion as at 31 December 2001.

The entire investment landscape has changed radically over the last two decades. Does this mean fewer opportunities and lower expected returns? Since the end of the 1970s, governments around the world have singled out inflation as the pernicious enemy that must be defeated at all costs. During the intervening two decades, they have been spectacularly successful in this aim, with inflation levels dropping significantly throughout the developed world. Yet investors are not universally happy, contrary to expectations. Many con-

tinue to hanker after the 'good old days' of high inflation, bemoaning the fact it is no longer possible to generate a satisfactory level of income. The prosperity bestowed by high inflation and high interest rates is, however, an illusion.

The priority of so-called 'income investors' is to generate sufficient income to leave their capital base intact. High interest rates may make their life easier in this regard, but there is a hidden cost. As inflation drives the price of goods in the shops higher, so the purchasing power of an investor's capital base is eroded. In short, whether it is the investor that eats into the capital base or whether it is rising consumer prices, the end effect is exactly the same. Thus it is the return that the investor achieves over and above the rate of inflation (the real return) that is important, rather than the level of absolute or nominal return.

After recent disappointing results, investors are waking up to the fact that the next decade is unlikely to be anything like as good as the last two. Falling inflation was the main driving force behind the strong performance of both bonds and equities through the 1980s and 1990s. However, with inflation now low and stable throughout the developed world, the scope for a further re-rating of financial assets has become increasingly limited. In other words, the 'easy money' has been made and future investment returns are likely to be much closer to their long-run averages.

Bonds were the unsung heroes of the 1980s and

early 1990s. Whilst their successful equity cousins had praise heaped upon them, bonds went quietly about their business, racking up equity-type returns with much lower volatility. During the period from January 1980 to December 1993, the US inflation rate fell dramatically from 13.3% to only 2.7%. This elicited a very positive response from the US bond market, which saw yields fall dramatically and investment returns skyrocket. The US bond market generated a total return of 376% in the period 1980-93 – an annual real return of 9%.

In the period since 1993, US inflation has stopped falling, with the result that real investment returns have also fallen. Furthermore, since that same period, the US bond index has produced a real return of only 4.2% per annum. In the 102 years from 1900 to 2002, UK government bonds have produced a real return of only 1.1%.

Bonds pay a fixed return and therefore offer no inflation-protection. Due to this, their sensitivity to rising inflation is relatively easy to understand. However, with equities the link is perhaps more difficult to fathom, particularly given that companies can protect their profits by raising the price of their end products. Yet high inflation is bad news for equities, because of its adverse impact on interest rates and economic stability. In addition, high inflation reduces the visibility of earnings and makes it difficult for investors to identify which companies are managing their affairs in a prudent and effective manner. In short, the risks associated

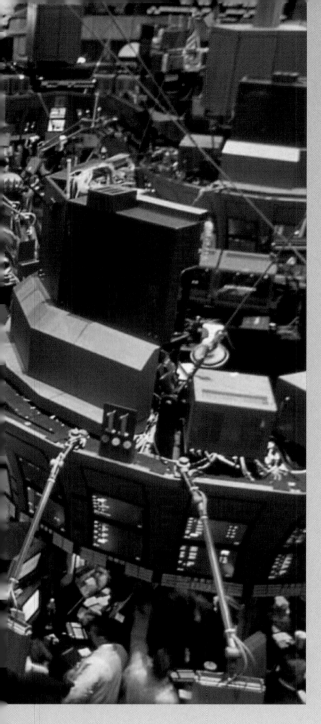

ASHBURTON

was significantly underpinned by changes in the inflation environment. The transition from high inflation to low inflation was pivotal to the re-rating and subsequent strong performance of financial markets at that time. However, this process has largely played itself out – inflation is now low and stable throughout the region and equity ratings are relatively high by historical standards. Indeed, if anything, they are a little too high in the United States. In short, investors are going to look elsewhere for high investment returns.

When the British people voted for the Conservatives under Margaret Thatcher, they did so out of desperation, driven by the dire state of the country's economy. The economic reform that followed – the abolition of exchange controls, privatisation, the promotion of competition and free trade and so forth – ultimately led to a renaissance in the fortunes of the United Kingdom. Who would have thought in the dark days of the 'Winter of Discontent' that, in just two decades, the UK economy would be regarded as being one of the most successful in the developed world?

Useful lessons can be derived from the UK experience for Japan. During the 1990s, whilst the West prospered, Japan floundered, weighed down by too much debt, outmoded management techniques and political inertia. In 2001, there were clear signs that the Japanese people had had enough and demanded change. Pro-reform candidate, Junichero Koizumi, was elected to the position of prime minister over the heads of the political elite and expectations ran high that Japan had finally turned the corner. Although many Japanese have grown impatient at the lack of progress on the reform front, it is important to remember that a significant proportion of the Thatcher reform programme did not emerge until several years after the 1979 election. At its recent low, the equity market was cheap by most yardsticks and investors were generally underweight – these are the usual preconditions for the start of any bull market. The economy may be in a parlous state, but that is generally the case at major turning points in the stock market.

Japanese share prices have recently risen strongly, with official data signalling that the economy has passed its worst point. At the very least, the Japanese equity market has probably embarked on a 1999-style cyclical recovery. If the people of Japan get their way and economic reform is indeed forthcoming, the outcome could well turn out to be substantially more profitable. Qualified, licensed experts with the appropriate track record and capable of making effective judgements at a macro-economic level, supported by a robust investment methodology, will continue to prevail in Jersey. This would apply to similar experts in any other financial centre, provided they could establish a positive relationship built on trust with their clients.

While time zones and fiscal structures play a part, this is work that can be done anywhere because the selection criteria are the same and we in Jersey are prepared to be measured against any other jurisdiction in the world.

John Major addressing the Ashburton seminar

Scottish Widows International

Gartmore Fund Managers International

Liberty Ermitage Group

with equity investment are proportionate to the level of inflation.

A general reduction in returns will present the investment industry with considerable challenges. With so much emphasis today placed on relative performance and benchmarks, most investment managers remain fully invested throughout the investment cycle. This mattered little when the markets were trending strongly upwards and passive 'buy-and-hold' strategies always eventually bore fruit. More recently, however, as investment returns have dropped and equity markets have struggled, investors appear to be increasingly dissatisfied with mainstream investment products. Although this may be an over-simplification, most investors assess performance in absolute terms, i.e. "how much money have I made?", whereas the typical investment manager thinks in relative terms, i.e. "have I outperformed the benchmark?" These two positions are only consistent so long as markets keep going up.

What are dissatisfied investors to do under such circumstances? The challenge now is to find an investment product that shares their objectives, which are likely to include the avoidance of loss and minimisation of volatility. The hedge fund industry is an increasingly popular avenue. Active funds, which have the ability to move in and out of cash, are a more conventional option.

The secular or long-term bull market in Western equity and bond markets of the 1980s and 1990s

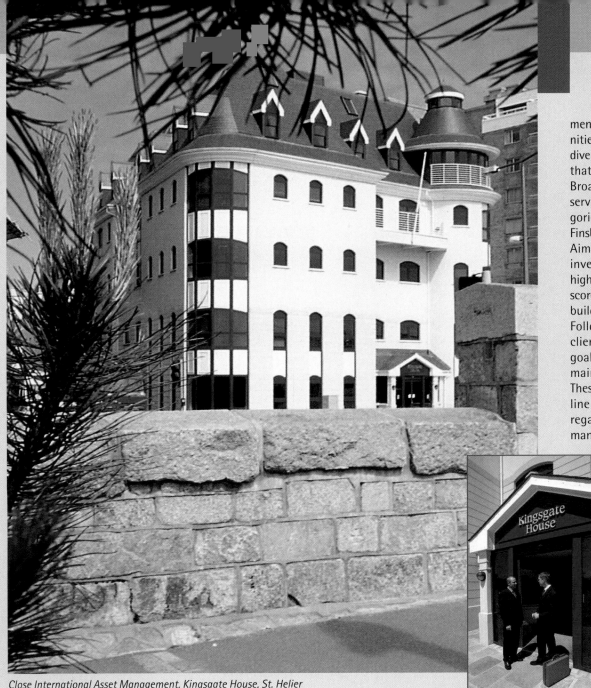

Close International Asset Management, Kingsgate House, St. Helier

Wealth management services with a personal touch

Close Brothers Group Plc. is one of the UK's leading independent merchant banking groups. Founded in 1878, the Group features among the 200 largest companies listed on the London Stock Exchange by market capitalisation. The Group's clients range from private individuals to institutions and charitable organisations.

Part of the Group's offshore operations, Close International Asset Management's head office is in Jersey, handling private clients and institutional investment management – always with a view to

bespoke services. The company takes advantage of the island's long-standing reputation as a growing yet strictly regulated international finance centre, enjoying good communications with Europe and beyond.

In the Channel Islands, Close offers a complete range of specialist financial services to the private client investment market. These services – available to an international client base – include investment management and dealing, in addition to various collective investment schemes. Through its sister companies in Jersey and Guernsey, Close has been providing a comprehensive range of wealth management services through a relationship-driven private banking approach for over 35 years.

Close International Asset Management recognises that few investors have the time or resources to successfully manage their own invest-

ments. The company therefore broadens opportunities available in the marketplace, by providing a diverse range of products and management services that cater to both small and large portfolios. Broadly speaking, its products and management services are covered by the following three categories: Personalised Portfolio Management, Close Finsbury Funds and Global Portfolios of Funds.

Aimed at the high net-worth and sophisticated investor, the Portfolio Management service is highly "personalised". This tailored approach underscores the Jersey-based company's commitment to build close and lasting relationships with clients. Following in-depth discussions to establish a client's financial circumstance and investment goals, assigned investment managers create and maintain a portfolio of approved investments. These can be enhanced or modified at any time, in line with a client's changing preferences, with regard to time horizons, risk tolerance, performance expectations and so on.

The Close Finsbury Funds are a range of collective investment schemes covering the world's leading stock markets and other specialist sectors, which enable moderate investors to build their portfolios. Uniquely, in a field where other companies often over-stretch themselves in their effort to manage investments globally, Close Finsbury succeeds by working from a flexible business model. If in-house expertise exists for managing certain funds, that expertise is called upon. In other cases though, fund management is outsourced to specialist companies with proven track records. Clients benefit from a comprehensive spread of investments and can rest assured that their best interests are always being looked after.

Lastly, the Global Portfolios of Funds service allows clients to diversify their investment according to chosen risk levels. Using funds from the world's leading investment managers, this flexible service provides discretionary asset management. A local investment committee determines the best allocation for a client's portfolio in terms of markets, assets and currencies. The ideal combination of funds for each portfolio is then worked out, after a rigorous selection process and due diligence. Quantitative and qualitative comparison of funds and their performance, and regular monitoring of every investment, enables Close to optimise portfolios over time. There are five portfolio options, ranging from defensive to aggressive.

When it comes to minimising risk and maximising returns, Close International Asset Management's bespoke services and philosophy of investment diversification ensure that clients are offered the right balance.

Investment management team

Managing Director, Nigel Hall

Relax in the certainty that your wealth is well managed

Investment management team

Bespoke offshore services

The offices of Aberdeen Private Wealth Management Limited, in St. Helier

Aberdeen Private Wealth Management Limited understands that many investors simply do not have time to construct and manage a portfolio of investments – or to assess investment opportuni-

ties, monitor market and currency movements and effectively control the day-to-day administration of their investment portfolio. With the emphasis on personal service, the company offer investors a real alternative to just handing over hard-earned assets to a faceless organisation.

"Most firms offering a private client service claim to provide a tailored package; but in practice this isn't always the case. We have a small team of locally based professional investment practitioners. They have many years' experience in the industry and are dedicated to providing an unrivalled, bespoke service," says Bruce Harrison, Investment Director. "They also have a full under-

standing of individual client needs and their expectations from an offshore environment."

Aberdeen builds a close working relationship with its clients, involving them in the design of their portfolio from the outset so that they feel part of the process. This often means meeting clients in person, in order to discuss attitudes to risk, return expectations and investment time horizon. In dealing with the specific financial affairs of each client, the company makes sure it understands fully their current financial position together with their objectives and future requirements. Experience has shown that a face-to-face meeting achieves this understanding, helping to build mutual trust and respect – which are all important in developing and maintaining a successful long-term business relationship.

"We also understand the need for timely and accurate reporting," says Bruce Harrison. "Using the latest in technology, clients are kept informed on a regular basis of the performance of their investments. Client records are held on our in-house system and are only accessible locally." Through this regular contact and reporting, the firm ensures that the portfolio always meets each client's changing needs. He adds: "After all, when you've worked hard to earn the money, it is comforting to know that someone else cares about it as much as you do."

The company adopts a conservative, not speculative, approach to investment – with a preference for capital preservation and secure steady growth over more high-risk strategies. Experience shows that this approach produces more consistent returns in the long term.

As a member of the Aberdeen Asset Management Group, the Fund Management team has access to group research on individual stocks, capital markets, currencies and economic trends worldwide. The Jersey team also collates information from international stockbrokers, fund management houses and other financial institutions. Taking into account the group views and balancing this with external research, it holds regular asset allocation meetings where recommendations are translated into strategies and action.

Those seeking bespoke offshore service will find that Jersey is an attractive proposition. It offers the benefits of a well-established offshore financial centre without the many risks associated with newer and less stable territories. The island is strictly regulated and only institutions of the highest reputation and integrity are permitted to establish new businesses and operate there. Modern laws and a comprehensive regulatory framework are in place, ensuring that the island maintains its reputation as a secure centre for investment. All investment businesses are regulated by the Jersey Financial Services Commission.

Ashburton's Global Investment Strategist, Peter Lucas, outlines the company's unique approach to investment management

A unique approach to wealth management

A conservative, low-risk approach to the creation and preservation of wealth and the consolidation of personal relationships with its clients: that is the foundation upon which the successful Ashburton philosophy has been built.

The company today boasts a 6,000-strong client base, spread across more than 60 countries, for whom it manages funds in excess of £1 billion. Headquartered in Jersey, it now employs over 90 people worldwide and has overseas offices in the Isle of Man, Cape Town, Durban and Johannesburg, as well as representation in Kenya.

Its core investment philosophy is based on a long-term approach. Fundamental aims are to preserve capital, minimise risk and volatility and achieve consistent results.

The company employs highly experienced investment professionals with excellent track records in the management of portfolios and funds. It believes that its investment managers should be able to exercise flair in the management of client assets and, consequently, individual managers have discretion in security selection within their sphere of responsibility. The investment team makes its own macro-economic analysis of global growth patterns, inflation, exchange-rate and interest-rate trends and allocates assets internationally in a meticulously controlled manner.

The origins of Ashburton lie with the company's two founding members, Derek Breed and Tim Bettany, who both lived in Kenya for many years. When they met, Derek already had 22 years of experience in finance and investment manage

The creation of wealth with meticulous care

ment. Tim, after qualifying as an engineer with Shell, had moved up the career ladder, via Harvard Business School, to merchant banking and the acquiring and running of public companies. It was clear that such skill bases were very complementary, as was their strong belief that clients must receive the highest level of personal service. In addition to the founders' customer focus, there was a shared thinking that good and consistent returns could be produced, avoiding risk and volatility. The key was to manage a truly international portfolio mixture of equities, bonds and cash/currency deposits – again something radically different from other investment houses that seemed determined to risk all for, more often than not, unguaranteed returns.

Since Ashburton's establishment in 1982, their approach has proved highly successful. The investment results achieved have equalled or

bettered those of many international investment managers, who have not offered the same security of a low-risk strategy.

The company's history of ownership stretches back to 1931, when Jersey General Investment Trust plc was formed. This was the first Jersey company to be quoted on the London Stock Exchange. It was de-listed in 1989, but its subsidiary, Jersey General Executor and Trustee Company Limited, which was established in 1935 as the first trust company in the Channel Islands, became the chief operating company in the trust division of Jersey General Group. The Jersey General Group acquired Ashburton in 1989.

The establishment of FirstRand International Asset Management Limited (FRIAM), which became effective from 1 July 2001, represents the culmination of a process which began in March 1998, when Rand Merchant Bank took an initial stake in the Jersey General Group. The name of the Jersey General Group was changed to FRIAM, shortly after the change of ownership was effected.

Ashburton is committed to providing the highest level of client service, with more than one third of the staff at the heart of the company's administrative centre employed in this area. Where appropriate, each client has access to a minimum of two dedicated staff – a personal administrator and an executive. Clients are also kept informed about significant developments by means of regular client communications, in addition to the normal valuation and statutory reporting.

Ashburton's co-founders, Derek Breed and Tim Bettany

Embracing the future with confidence: Managing Director Trevor Falle, CEO James Baudains and Directors Nicholas Lee, Dennis Phillips and Nicholas Taylor

Keeping pace with the latest developments, the company recently launched its new website, with over 160 pages of up-to-date information and more than 40 documents available to download online. Principal sections within the site include a company overview, daily prices, monthly fund commentaries and performance data and comprehensive information on the range of products and services available to clients. The site is regularly updated with the latest information, available to users 24 hours a day, 7 days a week. Investment seminars are another priority. The firm prides itself on the forging of personal relationships with each client where possible and holds over 30 investment conferences each year – to which both clients and their advisers are invited – in Kenya, South Africa, the Channel Islands, the UK, the Isle of Man and across Europe. Ashburton's directors always endeavour to attend these prestigious seminars in person and make themselves available to discuss any issues clients may raise. Speakers include the company's investment directors, global investment strategists and economic consultants. Over the years, a variety of world-renowned guest speakers, including former British prime ministers and chancellors, have also joined the company's presenters on the platform. The aim is always to inform, explain and debate both past and future prospects for the world's economies and financial markets.

The company recently celebrated 20 years in the investment management industry, during which it has established an excellent reputation for integrity. It believes this rock-solid foundation and credibility will serve as a springboard for the future. Today though, compared to the early years, Ashburton is an autonomously managed subsidiary of a world-class financial services organisation, employing some 35,000 people, which values greatly the success of Ashburton's philosophy and its plans to embrace the future.

Ashburton's investment team makes its own macro-economic analysis of global growth patterns, inflation, exchange-rate and interest-rate trends and allocates assets internationally in a meticulously controlled manner

A centaur in the museum's garden

The Millennium Mosaic

Solid gold torque, over 3,000 years old

The making of the island

Jersey Museum

Drawing room of the 19th-century Merchant's House

Agricultural exhibit

Remedies of yesteryear

Jersey's military past

The kitchen revolution

Modern art by Heath Hearn - one of three paintings to commemorate the 50th anniversary of social security in Jersey

Major Francis Peirson
By artist John Ouless

Barreau - Le Maistre Art Gallery

Sir Anthony Paulet by artist Marcus Gheeraerts and the 'Death of Major Peirson' by William Holyoake

'A Jersey Lily', portrait of Lillie Langtry by Sir John Everett Millais

Queen Elizabeth's visit to Jersey in 2001, by renowned local artist Jason Butler

A life's journey

Local personality Mike Stentiford by painter Philip Harris

Art for all tastes

'Mrs Langtry' painted by Sir Edward Poynter

Financial Regulation

Working to the highest international standards

The Jersey Financial Services Commission building in St. Helier

By Colin Powell, OBE,
Chairman, Jersey
Financial Services
Commission

Since the middle of the 20th century, Jersey's reputation as an international finance centre of world renown has grown inexorably and this has had a dramatic impact on the island's economy and its residents. Looking to the future, there is every reason to expect the finance industry will remain a dominant force for the continued well-being of the island.

The finance industry accounts for over 60% of Jersey's national income, and an even higher proportion of the island's tax revenues. It employs over 20% of the working population, and through the wealth generated has had an even greater impact on employment opportunities generally.

In the 1960s, the growth in the financial service activities relied heavily on business drawn from the United Kingdom and from British expatriates working and living abroad. Through the 1970s the finance industry became more and more international in its outlook. Jersey became increasingly well-known throughout the world as a secure finance centre with sound financial institutions working closely with the City of London.

Jersey was fortunate in that the collapse of two small local banks in 1970 had given clear warnings of the dangers of inadequately regulating the finance industry. The collapse persuaded the island authorities to go for quality and only license banks that were of international standing and in the world's top 500. One result of this policy was that at the end of the 1970s the island authorities, almost uniquely, refused to license BCCI – a bank that later gave rise to much heartache for the world's financial community.

Through the 1980s and the 1990s, and continuing in the 21st century, Jersey became increasingly important as an international finance centre serving the global financial community. The reasons for the island's continued success as an international finance centre can be summed up by five keywords: stability, security, respectability, flexibility and quality.

Stability

Jersey has political, economic and fiscal stability. There are no political parties, and the fiscal structure has remained essentially unchanged for over 60 years. The island's economic strength is reflected in the absence of public debt and a strategic reserve broadly equal to one year's tax revenues.

The island is a Crown Dependency, with allegiance to the British Monarch and a constitutional relationship with the UK that is based on centuries of custom and usage. Jersey has autonomy in its domestic affairs, which includes the right to determine its own fiscal policy.

The island differs from many other similar finance centres that offer the advantages of low tax: its standard and maximum rate of income tax of 20% has remained unchanged since September 1940. Indeed it has been a low-tax area for centuries. To secure the island's loyalty, successive monarchs granted Jersey charters that exempted the islanders from English taxes.

The island's increasing popularity as an international finance centre therefore did not arise because Jersey manipulated its tax rate to secure that end. Jersey became more attractive as other countries increased the burden of taxation on their individual and corporate taxpayers.

Jersey has had an established relationship with the European Union since 1973, when the UK became a Member State. Under the terms of Protocol 3, attached to the Treaty of Accession of the UK, the island is 'within' the EU Customs Territory for free trade in goods but is otherwise 'outside' the EU and in particular is not a part of the EU Fiscal Territory. The island's relationship with the EU for free trade in goods also extends to the wider European Economic Area.

Jersey is a party to the Organisation for Economic Cooperation and Development through the UK's membership of that body, and thereby the island is party to decisions of the OECD (such as the Codes of Liberalisation on Capital Movements and Invisible Transactions) unless an exclusion is specifically provided for. Currently the island is a party to the World Trade Organisation only in respect of trade in goods. This will be extended to trade in services, once the necessary domestic legislation to provide for this has been enacted.

Jersey issues its own currency notes and coins for domestic transaction purposes. The notes and coins have the same value as the UK's currency, which is also legal tender in the island. Jersey does not seek to exercise separate control over the island's money supply and through the monetary relationship with the UK the interest rates and exchange rates confronting island businesses and residents are the same as those experienced within the UK. The island is not subject to the EU monetary arrangements, but if the UK joins the European Monetary Union the interest and exchange rates set by the European Central Bank would likely be the relevant rates for the island.

Security and respectability

Jersey has built up a sound image by matching security for those engaged in legitimate business with respectability, by offering investor protection. It also provides financial regulation and anti-money laundering measures, of a high standard, in line with best practice in the international community.

Through the selection of business and the licensing of institutions of stature, plus a comprehensive and up-to-date legislative framework, the island has sought to ensure that it continues to present an international image of respectability. Legislation covering banking, insurance, collective investment funds, investment business and all crimes money laundering is equal to or exceeds international standards. In recent times legislation has been enacted covering the regulation of company and trust company service providers: in this the island is a leading-edge jurisdiction and is helping to determine international standards.

The Jersey Financial Services Commission is the body responsible for the regulation, supervision and development of the financial services industry in the island. The Commission was set up by statute in July 1998. Prior to that, regulation of the finance industry was performed by the Finance and Economics Committee of the States of Jersey, the island's Parliament, through its Financial Services Department.

The Commission's key purpose is to "maintain Jersey's position as an international finance centre with the highest regulatory standards." This it aims to do by reducing risk to the public; protecting and enhancing the island's reputation and integrity; safeguarding the island's best economic interests; and in pursuit of the above contributing to the fight against financial crime.

In support of this key purpose the Commission aims to be fully aware of international regulatory standards and their application to Jersey, and to ensure that all authorised entities meet fit and proper criteria. It also seeks to ensure that all authorised entities operate within international standards of best practice. Further goals are to identify and deter abuses of breaches of legislation, and to ensure the Commission operates effectively and efficiently.

The Board of Commissioners, which is the governing body of the Commission, is drawn from experienced and able people from within the island, and from the UK and Europe. One of the Commission's key objectives is to enhance the island's reputation as a well-regulated finance centre, playing a full and active part in cross-border financial regulation, anti-money laundering and the fight against terrorism financing. Through Jersey's contribution to the work of international organisations such as the Financial Action Task Force on money laundering and the Basel Committee on Banking Supervision, both directly through the Commission and separately through my role as Chairman of the Offshore Group of Banking Supervisors (a body of 19 offshore centres established in 1980), there has also been growing international recognition of the island's high standards.

Jersey has been recognised as a jurisdiction that is working to international standards by bodies such as the G7 Financial Stability Forum and the Financial Action Task Force on money laundering, and through several independent reviews of the island's regulatory standards.

Jersey offers security for those living in areas of political and economic instability looking for a refuge for their funds, particularly through the use of a Jersey trust. The island also pursues a policy of protecting confidentiality for legitimate business in the same way as other countries, such as the UK.

The island does not have bank secrecy legislation and – through its all crimes money laundering, investigation of fraud, insider dealing, and anti-terrorism legislation – the protection of confidentiality can be, and in practice is, stripped away where criminal activity is suspected and/or is subject to investigation. The island also is committed to adopt, in parallel with other jurisdictions, the principles of transparency and exchange of information – which are the cornerstones of current OECD and EU tax initiatives.

Flexibility and quality

One of the island's greatest strengths is the flexibility and quality of the services which it offers. This in turn rests on the range and level of skills and experience of the work force. Skills like these and the business acumen of Jersey residents continue to facilitate a process of change and the tapping of new business opportunities, such as the recent growth in the number of Special Purpose Vehicles, enabling the island to be remarkably

Jersey issues its own coins and banknotes, which have parity with UK currency

Jersey is internationally recognised for its impeccable financial standards

successful as what can be described as a "niche" market operator. This also has benefited from the close relationship that exists between the finance industry and the island authorities.

The quality of service provided also reflects the comprehensiveness of the commercial legislation, the influence of a sound regulatory system, the quality of the judicial system, the communication links and also the island's proximity to the City of London and other European finance centres. Jersey has a particularly strong complementary relationship with the City of London. Much of the business undertaken in the island is introduced by institutions with City offices, and most of the funds that are attracted to the island from the world at large find their way into the global financial markets through the City.

Conclusion

In the early days, the emphasis of the island's finance centre activities was very much on deposit taking and trust and company administration. Since then, the activities have widened and deepened to include global custody, treasury operations, security issues, captive insurance and a host of other banking, investment, insurance and legal services.

Over the past 40 years, the island's finance industry has come a long way. As at March 2002, there were just over 60 banking licences with bank deposits of £135 billion – an increase of 10.5% over the previous year. The number of collective investment funds was 353 with a value of funds in the island standing at £107 billion, an increase of 12.8% over the previous year. Taking all the funds that are managed in Jersey together, the figure well exceeds £300 billion – which for an island of 45

square miles and a population of less than 90,000 is a considerable achievement. There are also over 30,000 Jersey registered companies, and new incorporations each year of some 3,000.

The benefit Jersey derives from being an international finance centre is shared with the City of London and through the latter is of benefit to the UK economy. It is estimated that of the total funds managed in Jersey, more than £200 billion is invested in or through the City of London, and Jersey serves to complement many of the financial services provided in that location. In providing financial services, the island is also supportive of other European financial centres, such as Zurich, Frankfurt and Geneva.

Jersey will continue to apply international standards of financial regulation, anti-money laundering and combating the financing of terrorism. The island also is committed to present a favourable environment for business, to remain competitive and to retain its traditional ability to respond quickly and flexibly to business opportunities as they arise. The island's overall objective is to remain in the top division of international finance centres and to continue to be recognised as such by the international community.

There is expected to be a continuing demand for the quality services that Jersey provides, both from individual and corporate customers. And with a reputation for complying with international standards, the island expects to continue to benefit from a flight to quality. Jersey's future as an international finance centre is considered to be as secure as that for the City of London, Switzerland, Luxembourg, Hong Kong or Singapore – which are centres the island complements and/or competes with in the offer of financial services on a global basis.

PricewaterhouseCoopers, a global provider of auditing, accounting and advisory services, claims historical roots stretching back to the mid-19th century. Operating in more than 150 countries worldwide, the network of firms employs well over 100,000 people, all dedicated to helping their clients succeed by channelling knowledge and helping them to create value.

PwC is the leading firm of chartered accountants in Jersey, doing business with many important local, international and government clients. First established on the island in 1920, the company has occupied an office in the financial heart of St. Helier since 1975. An experienced and professional staff of around 160, providing audit, tax and advisory services, is able to offer a wide range of professional advice. The tax advisory and compliance practice can also provide a comprehensive range of services associated with the formation and administration of companies and trusts. Should the need arise, the firm can also draw upon the expertise of its extended network of offices worldwide.

Industry expertise is provided to different market sectors. To facilitate the effective delivery of expertise to the marketplace, the firm specialises in Consumer and Industrial Products, Financial Services; and Technology, InfoComm and Entertainment. Multi-disciplined teams, with extensive industry knowledge and experience, work with clients in each of these sectors.

Trust and corporate administration services are delivered through entities specially designed to satisfy clients' varied requirements.

Head office of PricewaterhouseCoopers, situated in the heart of the business district

Providing expertise, ensuring satisfaction

Partner Peter Yates and Senior Partner Philip Taylor

Head office, client reception area

Assistant Manager Morna McColl

Artist Katy Brown's 'Dreaming Grounds' art exhibition sponsored by PwC

The firm works closely with other PwC firms around the world in promoting a 'worldwide' service and contributes to many firm-wide initiatives which cover different jurisdictions. The company's European Private Banking/Wealth Management Survey, several of which have appeared since 1993, is widely recognised as an industry benchmark for private banks and wealth management institutions throughout the continent.

On the island of Jersey, the firm is well-known for its commitment to the local community. Over recent years, it has adopted a hands-on approach to the sponsorship of young people from a variety of different disciplines – such as the arts, music and sport. Examples include the popular PwC Jersey Young Musician of the Year competition and exhibitions for up-and-coming local artists. In the sporting arena, it has helped with the purchase of sailing boats, designed to meet the needs of budding, local yachtsmen and women. The company also sponsors a number of the many international performing artists who hold concerts in Jersey every year.

Recently ranked the leader in overall client satisfaction by an industry study, Pricewaterhouse-Coopers continues to underline its ability to remain ahead of the competition – whether in Jersey or on the global stage.

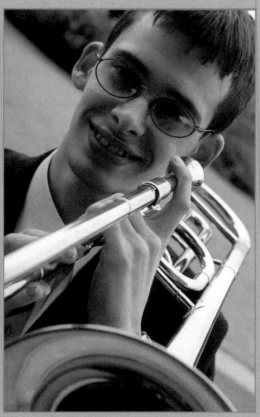
Dominic Palloy, young musician of the year, sponsored by PwC

Boats donated by PwC to St. Catherine's Sailing Club

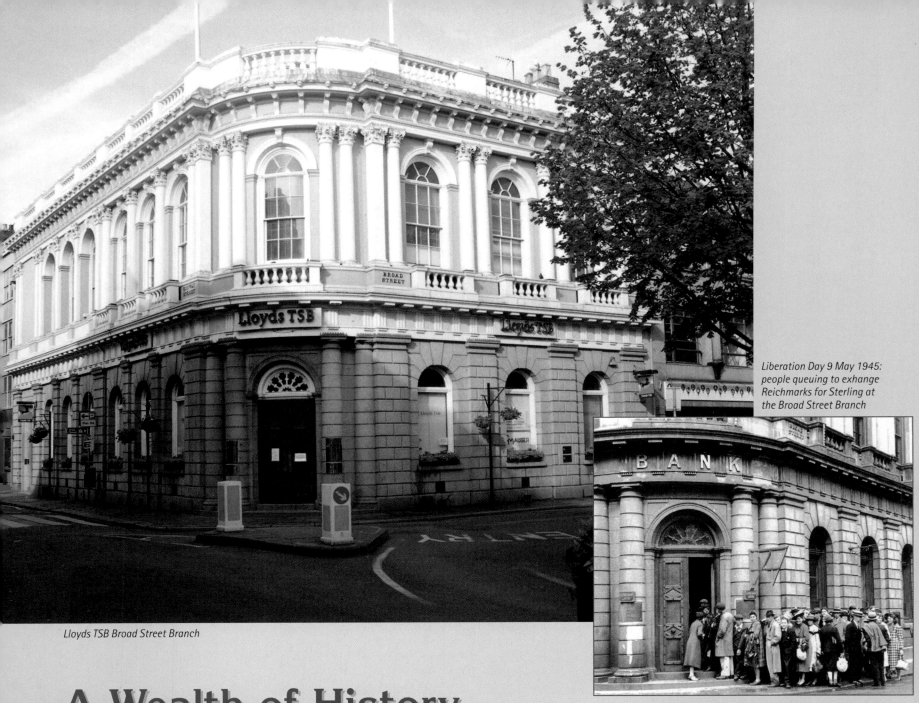

Lloyds TSB Broad Street Branch

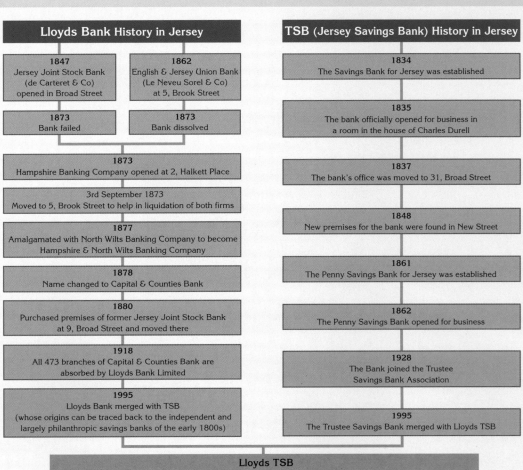

Liberation Day 9 May 1945: people queuing to exhange Reichmarks for Sterling at the Broad Street Branch

A Wealth of History on the Island

Lloyds TSB is one of the world's premier banking groups. It has a history in Jersey which stretches back to the early nineteenth century and is today one of the leading banks in Jersey's financial services industry. From this local base, onshore and offshore customer needs are dealt with on a daily basis by a professional and friendly team. Today, Lloyds TSB has an extensive branch network in Jersey for all your day to day personal banking needs, including mortgages, personal loans and saving facilities. There is also a dedicated Business Banking Centre for local corporate customers, together with a Jersey Offshore Centre for the specific banking and investment needs of expatriates worldwide.

Investing in the Island's Future

The local retail arm of the group in Jersey is investing heavily, with a major refurbishment of its Broad Street, St Helier branch.

The Broad Street building is listed by the Jersey Planning Department as a site of interest. Therefore, although Lloyds TSB will introduce the new corporate design, the bank will maintain the original character of the Broad Street building.

This investment will see Broad Street branch become the 'flagship' of Lloyds TSB retail banking in Jersey.

Lloyds Bank History in Jersey		TSB (Jersey Savings Bank) History in Jersey
1847 Jersey Joint Stock Bank (de Carteret & Co) opened in Broad Street	**1862** English & Jersey Union Bank (Le Neveu Sorel & Co) at 5, Brook Street	**1834** The Savings Bank for Jersey was established
1873 Bank failed	**1873** Bank dissolved	**1835** The bank officially opened for business in a room in the house of Charles Durell
1873 Hampshire Banking Company opened at 2, Halkett Place		**1837** The bank's office was moved to 31, Broad Street
3rd September 1873 Moved to 5, Brook Street to help in liquidation of both firms		**1848** New premises for the bank were found in New Street
1877 Amalgamated with North Wilts Banking Company to become Hampshire & North Wilts Banking Company		**1861** The Penny Savings Bank for Jersey was established
1878 Name changed to Capital & Counties Bank		**1862** The Penny Savings Bank opened for business
1880 Purchased premises of former Jersey Joint Stock Bank at 9, Broad Street and moved there		**1928** The Bank joined the Trustee Savings Bank Association
1918 All 473 branches of Capital & Counties Bank are absorbed by Lloyds Bank Limited		
1995 Lloyds Bank merged with TSB (whose origins can be traced back to the independent and largely philanthropic savings banks of the early 1800s)		**1995** The Trustee Savings Bank merged with Lloyds TSB
Lloyds TSB		

A winning combination

Michelle Molloy, head of client services

Private portfolio bond investment management

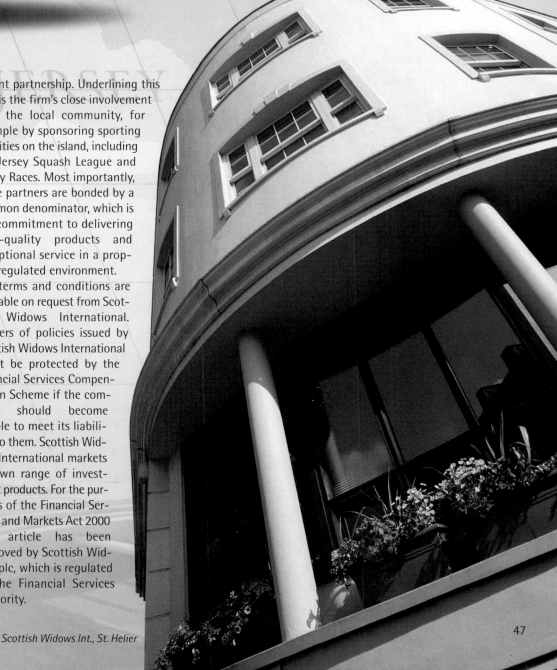

Scottish Widows International is the specialist offshore Life subsidiary of the Edinburgh-based Scottish Widows PLC, and has 140 UK sales consultants plus offices in Jersey, Belfast, Dubai and Cyprus. Launched in 1815 and now part of the Lloyds TSB Group, Scottish Widows has grown into one of the UK's largest and most highly respected financial institutions. It employs around 5,000 people and is responsible for managing client funds of around £78 billion on behalf of over three million customers worldwide.

Established in St.Helier in 1997, Scottish Widows International has a 30-strong staff which markets and sells a range of offshore bonds, aimed at investors around the world looking to maximise their potential for tax-efficient savings vehicles with good potential for growth over the long term. Those who purchase its International Investment Bonds, for instance, rely on the company to manage their investment across a range of funds. Private Portfolio Bonds allow clients to invest in a far wider range of assets, available on recognised stock exchanges and also from fund management houses across the globe. The firm prides itself on offering competitive prices and outstanding levels of service in this arena.

Both types of product facilitate tax planning for clients. A policyholder may benefit from tax deferral advantages by rolling gains up within the bond. The Private Portfolio Bonds also enable administrative gains, allowing policyholders to hold a range of products within one wrapper, not unlike a form of asset aggregation.

Scottish Widows International and Jersey form a potent partnership. Underlining this fact is the firm's close involvement with the local community, for example by sponsoring sporting activities on the island, including the Jersey Squash League and Jersey Races. Most importantly, these partners are bonded by a common denominator, which is the commitment to delivering high-quality products and exceptional service in a properly regulated environment.

Full terms and conditions are available on request from Scottish Widows International. Holders of policies issued by Scottish Widows International won't be protected by the Financial Services Compensation Scheme if the company should become unable to meet its liabilities to them. Scottish Widows International markets its own range of investment products. For the purposes of the Financial Services and Markets Act 2000 this article has been approved by Scottish Widows plc, which is regulated by the Financial Services Authority.

Scottish Widows Int., St. Helier

St. Helier looking north

48

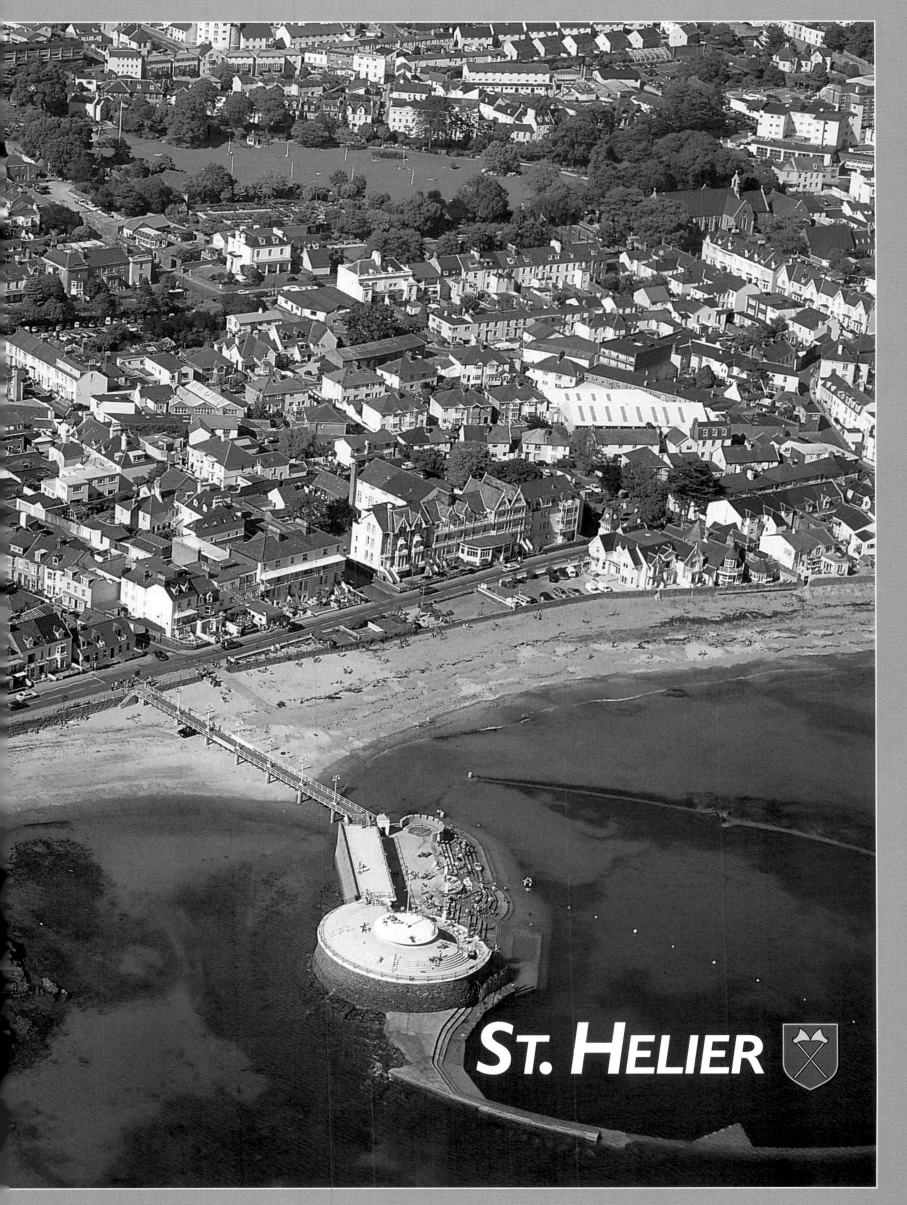

ST. HELIER

Royal Square

The statue of George II

Summertime

Relaxing at the Cock and Bottle

The United Club on Royal Square

ST. HELIER

The States Building

Town Hall

The Obelisk on Broad Street

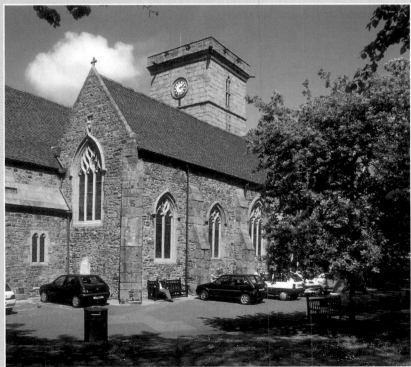
St. Helier Parish Church

Statue of General
Sir George Don

Banking
Keeping pace with international developments

By Hans Bärlocher,
Jersey Bankers Association

Banking has been the main foundation for the finance industry in Jersey throughout its 40-year history. The island, which first attracted international banking groups to its shores in 1961, is today home to some 60 banks from the United Kingdom, across Continental Europe, North America and South Africa.

The banks that operate here are those that are household names in their country of origin. Jersey has always insisted that banks that are granted licences are from the list of the top 500 banks worldwide in terms of capital strength. Measures such as these have helped the island to maintain its reputation for probity and quality, vital factors in the increasingly competitive international financial services arena.

The long-standing nature of the finance industry has enabled the banks to build up extensive knowledge and experience in handling international investors' banking and investment needs. One of the factors that first drew the banks to the sandy shores of Jersey was its adaptable regulatory regime, not to mention its favourable tax regime. In today's more rigorously regulated financial services market, the island – and the banking industry within it – has needed to adapt and embrace changes to its regulatory regime. The finance industry is aware that there are increasing calls for greater transparency in the field of international financial services, and so the banking and investment industry in the jurisdiction has been willing to work with the authorities, to meet these new, international demands. Jersey intends to remain at the forefront in the quality of its financial services business, a centre that other offshore jurisdictions would seek to emulate.

The island has played its part in the international drive to crack down on the manner in which terrorists might obtain their funding. Jersey was one of the first jurisdictions to follow the City of London with tough, new regulatory Orders which will result in terrorists' assets being frozen should any be discovered in the island's financial system. In addition, its anti-money laundering rules have been at the leading edge for some years. In more recent times, taxation regimes have come under the spotlight, with organisations such as the

Jersey - bankers to the world

Organisation for Economic Cooperation and Development and the European Union itself seeking to eradicate what they describe as "harmful tax measures". Many investors may find the various initiatives – from groups such as the OECD, the Financial Action Task Force and the European Union – confusing to understand. Where does the investor and the professional adviser fit into these developments and should they be concerned or reassured? It is worth reflecting on the regulatory changes and agreements that have been reached involving Jersey.

In 2001, the Financial Services (Jersey) Law was introduced. This extended the requirement of registration to trust and company service providers and imposed stricter regulation on their operation. The tightening of the rules in the trust and company area followed on from earlier legislation designed to regulate investment business in Jersey. Prior to that, the island was one of the first to introduce more wide-ranging anti-money laundering legislation, through the introduction of the Proceeds of Crime Law. Tackling financial crime has understandably become an ever greater priority since 11 September 2001 and Jersey, as I have outlined, was quick to act. Further regulatory initiatives have followed. Jersey became the first offshore international finance centre to secure an official Memorandum of Understanding (MoU)

with the German Securities Regulator. This agreement ensures mutual help and exchange of information for investigating securities offences such as insider trading, market manipulation and conducting financial business without a licence. The MoU is an indication of the international

recognition Jersey has for its willingness to cooperate with the leading Western governments in the fight against international crime. Similar MoUs have been established by Jersey with regulators in the United Kingdom, the Netherlands, South Africa, Belgium, Bermuda and, most recently, with the French regulators. In general terms, the banking industry in Jersey has been supportive of these measures, since it accepts and understands that quality regulation and an enhanced level of international cooperation, as well as the quality of products and services, will be amongst the priorities for the leading international centres and their clients in the future.

Jersey has also sought to reach agreement with the international authorities, where required. The OECD, for example, has published a "blacklist" of jurisdictions which it claims have a number of "harmful tax measures". Jersey was not included on that list, because the island reached an agreement with the OECD and committed itself to specific exchange of information.

However, the agreement has one very important proviso. The Jersey authorities' commitment to the OECD process is based on the essential need for a level playing field among all OECD member countries and also other non-member jurisdictions with which they are materially in competition in the provision of cross-border financial services. In other words, the Jersey jurisdiction will only enforce the OECD measures when and if competitor jurisdictions do the same. Under the agreement which Guernsey signed at the same time as Jersey, the two islands have confirmed they will reflect the OECD's principles of exchange of information and transparency both in a general political commitment and in tax information exchange agreements to be negotiated with individual jurisdictions.

There is certainly a drive towards a much more open and transparent financial environment across the globe and the latest measure in that category likely to affect the industry will be the European Tax Directive. The Directive relates to the taxation of the savings interest of EU residents within the European Community. The EU is seeking the cooperation of all the countries in the EU, dependent and associated territories such as the Channel Islands, Isle of Man and territories in the Caribbean, and named third countries, which include the USA, Switzerland and Monaco. Ultimately, under the proposal, each EU Member State would be expected to provide information to other Member States on interest paid from the Member State to individual savers resident in other Member States. This arrangement would also

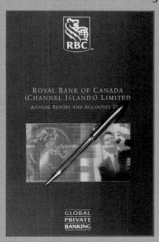

extend to the dependent and associated territories and the named third countries. The island's banking industry has been in close consultation with its Government in Jersey about the implications for its business. Together they have reached the decision that

Personalised financial services

exchange of information is the best way forward for the island. Jersey, therefore, has indicated it will go down this route – but once again, there are some important provisos.

Jersey is not expected to move ahead of anyone else. The EU Directive must also be adopted and implemented by EU Member States and the island has to receive sufficient assurances about the intentions of named third countries. Throughout this period of scrutiny, banks in Jersey have continued to develop their business and the island remains a thriving centre for banking and investment, with bank deposits continuing to rise. It is important to take into account other attributes that have helped Jersey reach this leading position as an international banking centre. The island's banks have always recognised the importance of innovation in their approach to client service. Many have invested in products and services tailored directly to the international investor, taking into account their specific needs. The benefits that arise as a result of the Internet explosion have also been adopted by many of the leading Jersey-based financial institutions. Without sacrificing the security of their services, banks have invested in new technology in order to deliver financial services via the desktop. There is no doubt that this trend will continue and it will be supported by a commitment to first-class client service, a hallmark of Jersey's financial services industry for many years. I questioned earlier whether the professional adviser and the investor need be concerned by international developments. The fact is that legitimate

investors need not fear the move towards greater transparency and the introduction of stricter regulatory rules to crack down on money laundering and financial crime. Indeed the reverse is true: investors can take comfort from knowing that their investments are located in an international financial centre of the highest regard, where great care is taken to maintain rigorous standards and to thwart financial crime. In the long run, greater transparency will benefit the legitimate investor by raising reputation and security standards.

Yet investors should take note of these far-reaching developments in financial services. We are finding that business is increasingly being attracted to the financial institutions and jurisdictions that focus on quality – both in the pedigree of the financial institution, the quality of the services, and the standing of the centre's regulatory regime. It is a combination that Jersey, with its stable political and economic history and solid reputation, continues to offer. This helps to explain why the island remains one of the most attractive locations for banking and investment.

Local knowledge, global experience

Friendliness and confidentiality

Allied Irish Offshore office in St. Helier

Allied Irish Offshore is a registered business name of AIB Bank (CI) Limited, which has been serving clients worldwide from its Jersey base since the early 1980s. It is a wholly owned subsidiary of Ireland's largest bank, Allied Irish Banks, plc, headquartered in Dublin. The AIB Group operates principally in Ireland, where it has some 280 branches, and in Britain, where it has been voted best business bank since 1994. The group also has a significant presence in the US and Poland.

In the Channel Islands, Allied Irish Offshore is situated in St. Helier, Jersey. The offshore subsidiary – which employs some 130 people – offers a wide range of products and services to its mainly international clientele. Among the offerings are private banking and portfolio management, with special emphasis placed on personalised products.

From Jersey, the company provides a range of corporate and credit services. Offshore mortgages are available to help customers in the purchase, remortgage or equity release of residential property. Further comprehensive services, suitable for expatriates, make the experience of leaving home and living abroad easier. They include assessments with clients of financial matters, such as payment and introduction to taxation experts. More personal products and services – among them life assurance, savings, investment, insurance and pension planning – can be arranged through introductions to specialist professional providers, and are geared to ensuring security and quality of life. When it comes to banking, Allied Irish Offshore provides a range of financial services combined with years of expertise. Customers, for example,

may avail themselves of fixed and instant access accounts, debit cards, foreign exchange, securities and fund transfers – all at competitive rates. Internet banking with the company also facilitates worldwide, 24–hour access to accounts and other services. Private banking, a key service, gives clients their own experienced personal private banker, supported by a team of skilled and dedicated individuals. After building a picture of individual requirements, the private banker is able to offer intelligent and effective guidance in the use of AIB Group's extensive range of services.

Through wholly owned trust subsidiaries, Allied Irish Offshore can assist in the formation and ongoing management of offshore companies. It can also establish and administer a trust – frequently used as part of tax-efficient and succession planning structures – and act in either a sole or joint capacity as trustee. The Corporate Administration area provides a range of services supporting the administration of employee benefits and share ownership schemes. Offshore fund administration, particularly for international hedge funds, is another growth business area. Fund management services, another major offering, allow customers to build their money and protect their wealth. These services include managed currency, money market and equity funds.

Last but not least, investment services are provided through a subsidiary company, AIB Portfolio Managers (CI) Limited, established in 1993. The services it provides complement those available from the bank and its other subsidiary companies. Two distinctive and highly personalised services are avail-

able: discretionary portfolio management and advisory portfolio management. Customers choose which decision process is best, depending on their level of activity and personal involvement in the investment.

Regular reviews of a portfolio, in terms of its composition, performance and expectations, ensure individual requirements are met. In all cases, the bank's investment philosophy is to broadly match an agreed relevant benchmark index, which is turned into an operational investment strategy for both the short and long term. To ensure investment management policy matches the AIB Group's high standards, the Jersey-based company is supported by investment management colleagues in Dublin and London. This is a measure of the professionalism and ongoing commitment to customer satisfaction of Allied Irish Offshore on the island.

Tiger Swimming Club, sponsored by AIB

A warm welcome to offshore financial services

Standard Chartered Grindlays was established in Jersey in September 2000, following the merger of Standard Chartered Bank and Grindlays Private Bank. A leading provider of offshore financial services, the combined entity offers real experience and understanding of local cultures as well as the advantages of belonging to the Standard Chartered Group.

Standard Chartered Grindlays provides an integrated, flexible range of offshore products and services to its international high net worth clients based worldwide, designed to preserve and maximise their wealth. The Bank has the experience and expertise to manage its clients' banking and investments, wherever they may be in the world, through five key product areas: banking, investments, foreign exchange, credit and trust services.

Banking services include interest-bearing instant access and fixed-term deposit accounts, cheque books and international debit cards. Standard Chartered Grindlays was the first offshore bank in Jersey to launch the popular international debit card, enabling clients to access their funds from anywhere in the world through ATMs and outlets displaying the VISA symbol.

Investment products include client-tailored advisory and execution-only services, plus privileged access to Frank Russell Company, a leader in the field of investment consultancy and management. Clients have access to the bank's foreign exchange services in all marketable currencies, dual-currency and principal protected currency deposits, forward exchange services and option forward contracts.

To assist with credit needs, the bank offers specialised lending facilities, cash-backed and investment-backed loans, UK mortgages, single premium investment bond-backed lending and interbank guarantees. Standard Chartered Grindlays Trust Corporation provides a full range of trust and corporate services with tailor-made solutions, including estate planning, taxation and long-term asset management.

Online services are especially popular with clients living or working abroad. "Checking balances, printing statements, ordering cheque books or transferring money from one account to another... these are just a few of the services our

The opening of the Hong Kong office

clients can benefit from without leaving the home or office, from anywhere in the world, at any time of the day," says Anthony Green, Internet Marketing Manager.

All clients have a dedicated Client Relationship Manager. To ensure consistency of knowledge and service levels, all Client Relationship Managers are required to undertake a structured training programme, which includes completion of the Securities Institute's Investment Advice Certificate. In addition, Client Relationship Managers are required to gain experience and knowledge of local markets. The aim is to provide personal service and advice to assist clients in finding the right products and services to match their individual needs.

Offshore offices in London, Dubai, Hong Kong, Singapore and Johannesburg help to extend the Standard Chartered Grindlays' global reach whilst providing specialist knowledge close to clients. "Working closely with our Group's global network," says Andrew Hunter, CEO Standard Chartered Grindlays, "we are well placed to concentrate on the needs of clients in the core markets of Asia Pacific, South Asia, Middle East and Africa. We are also able to continue to look after the needs of these clients if they move to other parts of the world."

Both Standard Chartered and Grindlays are fortunate to have a long history and strong brand franchise in their core markets. As the wealth of the Group's clients increases, typically they will wish to place a portion of their assets in a safe jurisdiction offshore with a bank that they trust. Standard Chartered Grindlays-Offshore Financial Services is well placed to assist these international clients with the preservation and maximisation of their wealth.

Standard Chartered Grindlays' headquarters in Jersey

GLOBAL REACH WITH LOCAL PRESENCE

UBS is the world's largest private bank, part of a leading financial organisation operating in over 50 countries and from every major international financial centre. The company's plan to expand its private banking presence aggressively in key European markets appears to be comfortably on track. Indeed, the focus is on becoming "the private bank of choice for wealthy people worldwide", rather than just holding its position as the biggest in the field.

In Jersey, UBS employs more than 170 highly professional staff, mainly dedicated to accommodating all the wealth management needs of an affluent international clientele. The island's cachet as a major world financial centre means that people from all over the globe are happy to know that their money is being handled there. UBS Jersey deals with three main categories of client. The first is the Jersey-resident, Jersey-domiciled wealthy citizen. The second comprises UK-resident, but non-domiciled clients, including foreign expatriates resident in Britain. The final category covers clients who choose to undertake their private banking business in Europe's leading offshore financial centre through local intermediaries. The last two categories represent the offshore market that has long been catered for and which still represents a good majority of the business.

Like a handful of other private banks, UBS has been shifting its emphasis from in-house products to an "open architecture" approach which aims to offer a selection of best-of-breed third-party investment products – a choice which is increasingly demanded by private banking clients. PaineWebber, the US broker-dealer acquired by UBS in 2000, was a pioneer of open architecture and developed two products – Pace and Access – that use open architecture for "long only" portfolio construction. Both products are available to UBS clients, albeit under new names: UBS Fund Advisory, UBS Managed Fund Portfolio and UBS Money Manager Access. One of the biggest changes in the private banking world has been the separation of product vending from relationship management. Not so long ago, a UBS client wanting to invest in an equity portfolio would have been offered only in-house fund management services. But this ties the fate of the banking relationship to the fund's performance, whereas the latest thinking highlights the importance of being on the same side of the table as the client – hiring and firing investment managers.

Welcome!

UBS private banking team

The products derived from PaineWebber enable client advisers in the UK to offer a range of 55 third-party funds in various portfolio combinations, designed to meet a range of requirements. Funds are selected by a research group in Zurich from a much wider palette of several thousand funds, filtered for size, risk, performance, volatility and so on. From this approved list, a separate UBS team in London undertakes portfolio construction and optimisation for all the European offices.

These templates, which may vary between countries – for example, to allow for a degree of home bias among clients – are the model portfolios in the adviser's armoury. A selection is then made for the client, following a careful check of his or her investment preferences and risk appetite. Although the process is highly technology-driven, the client adviser provides the human touch.

Should the client want to include in their portfolio other funds that are not among the best-of-breed, this can be arranged on an advisory basis. In this case, it is a portfolio strategy which is being sold rather than a fund service, whereby a client makes their choice from a list of funds. There is a separate portfolio management service for clients who want to be invested directly in equities.

"Open architecture does not itself give us a march on the competition," says Hans Bärlocher, local Head of UBS. "The key is the quality of research. It is the high quality and intensity of fund research, followed by skilful portfolio construction, that distinguishes UBS."

Fees for investment programmes include a notional annual management fee of 1.5% for the selection, management and reporting of the portfolio – which is usually discounted by the client adviser to around 0.75% – and the normal internal management charge of 1.1% to 1.5% included in the fund price. But there is no up-front sales charge, because UBS buys the fund at net asset value, under its arrangement with the fund-management companies.

The Fund Advisory, Managed Fund Portfolio and Money Manager Access products have recently been offered to UK-resident, UK-domiciled clients and are soon to become available to resident but non-UK-domiciled clients.

Although the bank offers a wide range of investment products, the aim is to focus not on specific products but on developing an overall plan that looks at all aspects of the client's finances – including cash positions, investments, businesses and pensions. UBS is a team of people to help clients devise wealth plans, deal with trust issues and determine the most effective tax.

The company decided to combine the best of what an independent financial adviser has to offer with the best that a bank and a fund manager has to offer, in order to have something unique in the marketplace. The bank also aims to stand out from its competitors by offering clients more personal attention, based on a lower ratio of clients to advisers.

Although private banking is very competitive, UBS believes it has no direct rival in its bid to become a pan-European player.

The US investment houses have not shown long-term commitment to the region and tend to shift focus when the weather gets a little rough. At the same time, local boutiques cannot offer a broad, holistic service.

And the other major European banks are wooing a much wider clientele that includes the mass affluent, while UBS is pitching to the upper layers.

Historically, the private banks have been strong in the offshore market and in their own home market. Yet none have set down roots in several onshore markets, says one independent British consultant, adding that "if anyone can make this expansionist strategy work, it is UBS".

Serving investors worldwide

St. Helier

Central Market, opened in 1882

I told you to turn left!

Wests Centre

Dancing the night away

The ever-popular Bastille

Victoria Park

Central Market

The Blue Fish Cafe

The Opera House

Procession, by artist Jason Butler

St. James Art Centre

59

Elizabeth Castle

The 16th-century Elizabeth Castle

Preparing to fire the Signal Gun

Cannon battery

The Mount

The Parade Ground

Time for inspection

The 6th-century Hermitage of St. Helier

St. Helier's bed at the Hermitage

Castle defences

Military Museum

A commitment to the Channel Islands

The Channel Islands have become a major business centre for Clerical Medical's offshore operations, which are based in the Isle of Man. Today a leading provider of flexible and efficient investment solutions for individuals, companies and trustees – both in the UK and internationally – the company has enjoyed over fifteen years of continual growth and development in offshore operations, an area in which it is market leader. It also has a history of financial strength, reliability and stability – core skills that investors have come to depend upon.

The firm's business dates back to 1824, when the Clerical Medical and General Life Assurance Society was founded in the UK to serve the needs of clergymen and doctors. Whilst its story is one of enormous change, its core values and commitment to professionals remain the same. These are just as relevant now as in the days of Queen Victoria, the company's most famous policyholder.

That history of business evolution within the UK has been replicated with the company's activities in the Channel Islands. Clerical Medical first established an office in Jersey in the early 1960s. At that time the company offered a range of life and pension products, to meet the needs of Jersey and Guernsey residents.

Parallel to Clerical Medical becoming established in Jersey, the Island was becoming established as a high-quality centre for offshore financial services. As Jersey developed into an internationally renowned business centre, so Clerical Medical evolved its products and services to meet the needs of the Island's new customers. The local residents of Jersey and Guernsey continue to be attracted to the firm's products, although the vast majority of its business is now in connection with the overseas customers of the local finance community.

Clerical Medical is part of the HBOS Group, created when the Halifax Group and Bank of Scotland merged. HBOS plc is the eleventh-largest company in the UK and has total group assets of over £300 billion. In a dynamic and highly volatile market, financial strength is increasingly the key to meeting policyholders' expectations.

One of the main attractions of the Group's international investment products is that they offer access to Clerical Medical's offshore with-profits funds. With-profits, as an investment concept, has

Jersey office of Clerical Medical in Wests Centre, St. Helier

been at the core of the company since the 19th century. A with-profits fund is made up of shares in companies in the UK and overseas, property and fixed interest investments, together with a small proportion in other types of investment including cash. With-profits investment has a unique feature called smoothing. Smoothing aims to reduce the effect that fluctuations in the stock market can have on the value of investments, whilst still allowing the potential benefits from the higher returns expected from stocks and shares over the longer term. An offshore with-profits fund therefore effectively reduces the element of risk associated with stock market investment.

As part of the company's own commitment to the

Channel Islands, it is continually developing its presence in the region by upgrading resources of both people and infrastructure. In this way, it will continue to meet the needs of all its customers, both old and new, by offering a high-quality and comprehensive level of service on their doorstep. This move, coupled with the ability to offer a comprehensive product range tailored to the investment needs of the international market place, puts Clerical Medical at the forefront of offshore investments.

Personal service

Offshore head office in the Isle of Man

Wests Centre office

FIRST-CLASS OFFSHORE SERVICES

Bank of Scotland International, in New Street, St. Helier

Now Britain's fifth-largest bank, HBOS (Halifax Bank of Scotland) Group came into being after the merger of Halifax plc, the UK's leading mortgage provider, based in West Yorkshire and Bank of Scotland, the Edinburgh-based clearing bank.

The two banks have merged their former offshore operations in Jersey, the Isle of Man and Hong Kong – among the world's most reputable and well-regulated offshore centres – into a single business better equipped to compete with the traditional offshore banks. Trading as Bank of Scotland International, its registered office and principal place of business is in Jersey. The focus is on growing relationships with clients, by delivering value for money, high-quality service and absolute transparency.

A range of accounts are offered in sterling, US dollars and euros. Clients can choose from accounts that offer instant access, notice periods and current accounts. For guaranteed returns, they may select from various fixed-rate accounts in all major currencies. Also available are property and lending services, plus those related to investments, taxation and wealth-management. Specialist banking services enable clients to create a solid foundation for their finances.

The Offshore Mortgage Service provides mortgage finance for the purchase of properties in the UK, for residential or investment purposes. Benefits of an offshore mortgage include expertise, advice and help with specific requirements, credit for international investors, and potential tax savings.

Bank of Scotland International can assist with property purchases through offshore companies or trusts, and thus maximise tax efficiency. Access to expert tax advice – for property, residency and rental income issues – also enables it to arrange client-specific mortgages. The Jersey-based company helps professional people from all over the world move successfully to the UK, permanently or temporarily, through practical advice and tax-efficient financial solutions. If a client is living and working in the UK, but does not view it as a permanent home, offshore banking can minimise his tax liability. By setting up and using offshore bank accounts, investments, companies or trusts, the company can reduce or remove liability to various forms of UK tax. The management of private wealth is an important part of the offshore specialist's business. It therefore provides solutions for the preservation and growth of wealth for present and future generations.

The use of a trust or company can provide a number of tax and estate planning benefits. A sister company, Bank of Scotland Trust Company (International) Ltd, offers the full range of relevant services designed to meet the needs of non-UK citizens living and working abroad.

The principal benefits of using a trust include protection and preservation of assets for future generations, tax and estate planning including mitigation of inheritance tax, income tax and capital gains tax, avoidance of probate formalities and succession laws, distribution of assets at pre-determined times, and succession planning. Those who have set up a trust can also look forward to protection against political uncertainty, as well as continuity or professional asset management.

Products and services offered by the company make the most of offshore tax planning opportunities. For example, for all banking and savings products, interest is paid gross without the deduction of tax. Clients, however, will need to include interest when assessing income for tax purposes in their country of residence. The company can refer clients to a specialist accountancy firm for tailored advice.

Bank of Scotland International combines all the assurances and familiarity of the brand of banking that clients know and trust, with enormous worldwide experience and expertise in the offshore field. It provides attractive investment opportunities, with the high standards of service and the reputation of the combined forces of Halifax and Bank of Scotland.

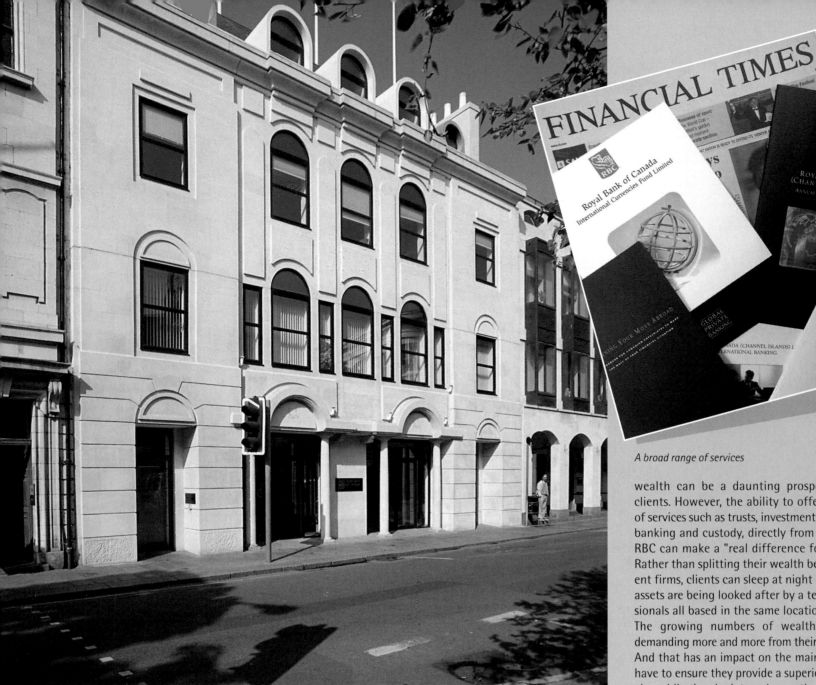

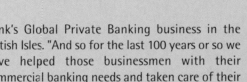
A broad range of services

Royal Bank of Canada Global Private Banking's Jersey Broad Street Office

A COMMITMENT TO QUALITY

Royal Bank of Canada has become one of the leaders in the business of helping wealthy individuals find the answer to their very specific needs. The group's operations based in the Channel Islands, which form part of Royal Bank of Canada's Global Private Banking network of private banking offices around the world, employ over 950 people, and has its Jersey offices in St. Helier's central banking district.

The Jersey office believes its quality of service – not to mention its highly professional staff and continual focus on providing tailor-made solutions – sets them apart from the competition. Clients can access services such as trusts for transferring wealth to the next generation, as well as investment management for income or long-term capital growth. Long-term financial goals can be achieved through the Bank's custom-made private banking solutions.

Founded in 1869 by a group of merchants in Halifax, Nova Scotia to help facilitate their trade, Royal Bank of Canada has grown to become Canada's largest financial services company and one of the world's leading banks. "As trade grew outside Canada's borders, so did the Bank. This allowed us to be close to our clients," says Philip Brewster, Senior Vice President in charge of the

bank's Global Private Banking business in the British Isles. "And so for the last 100 years or so we have helped those businessmen with their commercial banking needs and taken care of their personal wealth."

From his office in Broad Street, Brewster looks out on a business that is as focused today on meeting the needs of its high-net worth clients as it was a century ago. He acknowledges that managing

wealth can be a daunting prospect for some clients. However, the ability to offer a full range of services such as trusts, investment management, banking and custody, directly from Jersey, means RBC can make a "real difference for the client". Rather than splitting their wealth between different firms, clients can sleep at night knowing their assets are being looked after by a team of professionals all based in the same location.

The growing numbers of wealthy clients are demanding more and more from their private banks. And that has an impact on the main players, who have to ensure they provide a superior level of service while they look to enhance their capabilities. "We may be one of the largest providers of private banking services in Jersey, but we can't afford to rest on our laurels," adds Brewster.

To meet this challenge head on, the company has built a single, seamless business across the Channel Islands, in order to harness the full extent of its wealth management capabilities and to bring immediate benefits to clients and their advisors. The new larger and more robust administration capability allows relationship managers to spend more time servicing clients rather than handling paperwork.

Quality of service is key to success in private banking, and Royal Bank of Canada's Global Private Banking network seems committed to keeping ahead of the chasing pack.

Private banking hall

Creating peace of mind

The island's premier provider of security solutions, Securicor Jersey Limited has grown significantly over recent decades. Part of the global Securicor group, it set up on the island in 1970 and today has some 400 employees. It provides a full range of services to local homes and businesses, often 24 hours a day, all year round.

The company operates from purpose-built premises, on the Rue des Pres Trading Estate, north-east of St. Helier. Its eight main divisions – Locksmiths, Alarms & Monitoring, Guarding & Patrols, Fire Extinguishers & Training, Secure Storage, Cash Services, Parcels & Courier, and Cleaning Services – offer an ever-increasing

Lock up time

number of high-quality security solutions to all sectors of the island community.

The company is focused upon understanding the individual needs of customers to ensure that it provides real-time, customised security solutions that are flexible and responsive in the face of changing environments and growing global pressures. It believes in setting standards, not just following them, a strategy that allows the company to build a lasting partnership with its customers.

Underlining its dedication to customer satisfaction, Securicor Locksmiths recently joined forces with Abloy Security – for which it is the local official supplier – to devise a custom solution to secure the massive oak door at the entrance to Elizabeth Castle. Securicor, in conjunction with Abloy products, which range from tough mechanical locks to sophisticated electronic access control and locking systems, helps to secure virtually every major visitor attraction on the island.

The numerous services associated with providing electronic security solutions are handled by Securicor Alarms, which is at the forefront of technological innovation and expertise. This division's philosophy is based on the wider view that such systems are not simply about keeping unwanted intruders out: they should also make life easier, safer and more comfortable for homeowners and businesses alike. Their purpose is to eliminate personal risk, reduce costs and provide peace of mind. Day or night, the Securicor Alarm Receiving and Communication Centre is there, monitoring systems 24 hours a day, helping to keep property safe and to protect the Jersey way of life. If

the worst should happen – when every second counts – it will take immediate action, based on a pre-agreed, customised response strategy. The centre can immediately alert the appropriate emergency service, such as police or fire, or dispatch a Securicor First Response Officer from the Guarding and Patrols division. Office space is at a premium in Jersey, so many businesses have turned to the company's Secure Storage division. It offers a purpose-built secure archive storage facility aimed mainly at the business community and can store everything from paper documents to magnetic media. Should customers require their documents or data, the advanced document management database, together with the wide infrastructure available to Securicor, can have them delivered at any time, 24 hours a day, 365 days a year. Customers are also offered a secure document destruction service.

With over 30 years' experience in Jersey, Securicor Cash Services is responsible for carrying over £1.5 billion each year within the island – including an average of one tonne of coinage each working day. Amongst the other cash-related services, it currently processes in excess of £140 million per annum. The Fire Extinguishers division, besides supplying, installing and maintaining equipment, also provides potentially life-saving training in the use of extinguishers.

For a swift, reliable and trouble-free collection and delivery service, Securicor's local, national and international courier and freight services span the world. They provide next-day delivery to the Americas and many other destinations. One of Jersey's largest contract cleaning companies, Securicor Cleaning offers a full range of services to homes or businesses across the island.

Securicor Jersey offers support at all levels, to everyone from individuals to global players. By providing

Document storage and record management facility

customers with security solutions that encompass the Securicor core values of reliability, integrity and innovation, the company remains dedicated to ensuring homes and businesses around Jersey enjoy real peace of mind.

Serving the people of Jersey 24 hours a day

A shoppers' paradise

Bustling King Street

Crystal, the ideal gift

Beautiful Jersey pottery

Clothes for the discerning at De Gruchy

Latest European fashions

Aurum, Jersey's leading jeweller

Sale time!

De Gruchy, Jersey's premier department store

A sense of style

The elegant interior

A *family tradition*

Alexa, Richard and Julie Blampied

Founded some three decades ago in St. Helier, Aurum Manufacturing Jewellers offers a wide range of original, elegant and hand-crafted items. The company is owned and run by Jersey-born Richard Blampied. His early training included a spell at a prestigious goldsmiths' school in southern Germany, complemented by studies in the setting of precious stones. Today Aurum, the Latin name for gold, is very much a family business. Daughter Julie is a qualified gemmologist, while Richard's wife Alexa works as a designer and has reached the final stages in the De Beers Diamonds International Awards design competition. This experienced team operates from a workshop at its Charing Cross premises, an attractive listed building. The Aurum shop opened to the public in 1971. It includes a large showroom, where helpful staff are always on hand to offer advice to customers. The workshop – which also functions as a proving ground for local apprentices – is home to a trio

of goldsmiths, a gem setter, a jewellery repairer and designer. A quick glance around the room reveals a range of hand tools that would be familiar to craftsmen down the ages. It takes many years to master them all, so patience here is not so much a virtue as a necessity. Yet the beautiful jewellery turned out by these Jersey artisans is a testament to their skills and dedication.

Produced from the finest gold, silver and gemstones, Aurum's jewellery is always unique and individually crafted. It spans everything from traditional pieces to the very modern, sometimes especially commissioned by customers. Staff are always happy to talk through a new design. This close collaboration, which may include several detailed colour sketches, ultimately results in a simple vision being turned into resplendent reality. Handmade objets d'art, exhibited in the showroom, underline the craftsmen's breadth of experience and artistry. Some take many years to create, such as the sterling silver replica of the 18th-century British warship, the HMS Victory, mainly the work of Richard Blampied. Over the last decade, the firm has also produced a number of silver trophies for competitions held worldwide. It also achieved a real coup in 1989, making an 18ct gold-plated sterling silver scale replica of the mace used by the Bailiff of Jersey, a piece proudly presented to the Queen when she visited the island.

In recognition of the firm's high-quality work, Goldsmiths Hall in London awarded Aurum a registered Assay mark, which includes the initials (REB) of its founder. It is also a member of the National Association of Goldsmiths. Richard Blampied himself is a Freeman of the City of London and a Freeman of the Worshipful Company of Goldsmiths – a body responsible for hallmarking precious metal articles and promoting excellence in the design and craftsmanship of silver and jewellery.

The sheer range of jewellery on offer stems in part from the firm's extensive collection of precious

Aurum, the diamond specialists

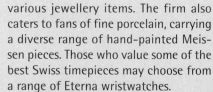

Qualified gemmologist Julie Blampied

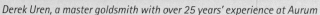

Derek Uren, a master goldsmith with over 25 years' experience at Aurum

stones. They include unmounted sapphires, rubies, emeralds and diamonds. The majority of gems are purchased directly, such as from originating mines in the Far East or from reputable dealers.

Besides making its own jewellery, the firm also offers pieces that are imported from countries such as England, Germany and Italy. Each of these items is hand-picked by Richard Blampied during his European purchasing trips, to ensure the finest quality standards are maintained. Cultured pearls, which are carefully selected from the best of the "pearl harvest", are available for incorporation into various jewellery items. The firm also caters to fans of fine porcelain, carrying a diverse range of hand-painted Meissen pieces. Those who value some of the best Swiss timepieces may choose from a range of Eterna wristwatches.

As the venue for elegant modern, locally crafted jewellery, Aurum is often one of the first ports of call for both locals and visitors to Jersey. All appreciate the firm's long-held philosophy: "It doesn't have to be expensive… it just has to be good."

Jewellery for all tastes and pockets

The Aurum retail showroom and workshop, situated in historic Charing Cross

Designer Alexa Blampied

Luxury and *comfort*

The Hotel de France, situated on the outskirts of St. Helier, the capital of Jersey, is the largest hotel in the Channel Islands. Boasting historical character and style, it also supplies the comfort and facilities expected by today's guest – whether conference delegate, businessperson or holidaymaker.

In 1866 the Imperial Hotel, as it was known then, opened its doors to the public on the present site, but it was far too grand an establishment and closed in 1880. For the next 60 years it became Maison St. Louis, a Jesuit College for students studying theology, philosophy and science.

The German forces occupied the island in 1940 and Maison St. Louis became a training school for German NCOs. When Jersey was liberated in 1945, the property remained empty for eight years. It was then purchased by the Reynolds family and opened in 1954 under the present name, the Hotel de France. The current owners, the Parker family, purchased the hotel in 1971 and extended it considerably over the following years. A new wing was constructed, together with extensive conference rooms, banqueting kitchens and a new indoor swimming pool.

Over the last decade, the Hotel de France has undertaken a continuous series of major refurbishments, resulting in the splendid establishment as it stands today. The original first-floor reception, for instance, has been moved to its present ground-floor position.

The hotel comprises 320 bedrooms, including eight Master Suites and six Junior Suites. Guests have the choice of two restaurants, with the Gallery offering fine à-la-carte dining and the newest development, the Atrium, providing informal dining together with a cosmopolitan bar, relaxed mezzanine lounge and boulevard café. The hotel has both indoor and outdoor swimming pools, a whirlpool spa with sauna, solaria and steam room, a hair and beauty salon, an extensive fitness centre with squash courts and a shop producing its own chocolate products aptly named after the original college, Maison St Louis. Leisure facilities even include an on-site cinema complex and a Photographic Museum.

The venue for many major conferences, the hotel offers an extensive choice of 20 superbly equipped meeting rooms suitable for groups from eight to 1,000. The largest is the Great Hall, which can seat 1,000 people in theatre style and hosts many spectacular themed gala banquets, both international and local.

The Hotel de France welcomes a diverse range of guests. They include British and continental delegates for conferences and incentives (from the pharmaceutical, financial and IT industries in particular), corporate clients who commute to Jersey weekly, leisure guests from all over the world staying mostly in the summer months, as well as an ever-increasing number of guests who take shortbreaks during the winter.

Both the hotel and Jersey welcome the challenge of sustaining and increasing the awareness of a unique destination, one which draws many guests back year after year.

Trusts in Jersey

Securing the future

By Robert A. Christensen,
Managing Director,
Volaw Trust Company

Jersey trusts provide a secure home for international clients' assets

The legal concept of a trust dates from English medieval times. Essentially it is a means of separating legal ownership of assets from those that enjoy them by conferring legal title to an independent third party. The trust concept has been developed over the centuries and trusts are frequently used in effective tax and estate-planning arrangements.

Whilst trusts were first given legal recognition by courts exercising their equitable jurisdiction to enforce the terms of trusts, Jersey has given statutory recognition of trusts with the Trusts (Jersey) Law 1984.

This law provides a modern legal framework for establishing trusts in Jersey and for protecting beneficiaries. The island was the first jurisdiction to introduce licensing and regulation of pro-fessional trustees under the Financial Services (Jersey) Law 1998. Often used to protect assets from punitive tax regimes, trusts may also protect the assets of professional persons against speculative litigation. Or they may provide security for assets potentially open to expropriation or confiscation by a politically unstable or hostile regime.

A Jersey trust is a useful vehicle in which to hold substantial family wealth in a politically stable jurisdiction. It is also used for estate planning and, as a trust may continue in existence after the settlor's death, it can provide for continuity in ownership and management of a family's property.

Trusts are often more effective and offer greater flexibility for complex arrangements than a will. A trust can help avoid probate formalities and harsh succession laws in the settlor's country of residence: Jersey law offers particular assistance to those establishing a Jersey trust for avoiding foreign rules of forced heirship. In certain circumstances a Jersey trust can be used to defer or avoid both income and capital taxes, which would otherwise be payable on assets if they were held in the settlor's country of domicile.

Trusts are increasingly used in employee-benefit planning. Various plans – including executive share option schemes, employee share purchase plans, deferred bonus plans and pension schemes – use trusts to protect employees' benefits. Many such plans are established in Jersey, which provides a tax-neutral environment for their operation.

Trusts may also be suitable structures for charitable reasons; specific purposes; employees working abroad; shared investment schemes; avoidance of exchange controls; and as special purpose vehicles for structured finance transactions.

A trust is created when a person (the 'settlor') transfers certain assets to one or more persons ('trustees') on the understanding that the trustees will hold and use those assets for the benefit of other persons ('beneficiaries'). The terms of trust are usually set out in a written trust document. The assets of a trust typically comprise money, shares in companies and other tangible or intangible moveable property.

The trust document lays down the foundations of how trustees are to administer and manage the trust assets and how they are to distribute and dispose of trust assets during the trust's lifetime. In general, the settlor of a discretionary trust (which allows trustees to decide how they exercise some of their powers in relation to the trust)

Centurion Trust Group

Volaw Trust Company

Protecting family wealth

Employee share ownership plans

provides trustees with a letter of wishes. Though not generally legally binding, the letter gives trustees guidance as to how the settlor wishes them to exercise their powers and discretions. A discretionary trust arrangement may allow for a protector (usually a professional person well known to the settlor) to be appointed to oversee the exercise of specified powers and discretions. The protector may also remove trustees and appoint new ones in their place.

Trustees have a fiduciary duty to act in accordance with a trust deed and in the interest of beneficiaries. But if a settlor retains control of the assets, or issues instructions to trustees which are accepted, it could be deemed that the trust was not properly settled in the first place, thus rendering the trust invalid.

Most trusts are established by a written document that sets out the duties and powers of trustees. They generally take the form of a settlement or a declaration of trust. A settlement will be entered into and signed by both the settlor and trustee, thus providing clear evidence of the intentions of both parties and of the agreed obligations assumed by the trustee. A declaration of trust is entered into and executed by the trustee only, and records that the trustee has received certain property, specified in the document, to hold upon the terms set out in the document.

It is sometimes more convenient to create a trust by declaration of trust rather than by settlement. For example, the settlor may not be available to sign the document, when it is prepared. Moreover, a declaration of trust does not name the settlor, thus preserving the confidentiality of the source of the trust assets.

There is no requirement to register with any authority the creation of a trust in or subject to the law of Jersey; nor is a copy of the trust

instrument available for public inspection. A trust therefore remains a private agreement between the settlor, trustees and beneficiaries. Moreover, there are no stamp duties or other fiscal charges payable on establishing a trust.

There are several types of trusts, the most widely used being the discretionary trust – especially in the Channel Islands. This type allows considerable scope in the nomination of beneficiaries and the appointment of the trust fund between beneficiaries.

A special form of discretionary trust is the accumulation and maintenance trust, whose income is either accumulated or paid out for the maintenance, education or benefit of children or other minor beneficiaries. In the UK, it qualifies for particularly favourable inheritance tax treatment and is ideal for parents wishing to benefit their

children. In fixed interest trusts the trust document defines the rights of beneficiaries from the outset. The trustees do not therefore have any discretion as to the assets' distribution. An example of this type is the interest in possession trust, where a person, often the settlor, receives the trust fund's income during his or her lifetime, following which the trustee is required to distribute the trust's capital to the capital beneficiaries defined in the trust document. Protective, or asset protection, trusts grant a fixed interest to the beneficiary, which changes into a discretionary arrangement so as to protect the trust's assets if the beneficiary faces financial ruin or speculative litigation. Other common types of trust include unit trusts, whereby members of the public pool their funds for investment through the trust; charitable trusts that benefit society rather than individuals; non-charitable purpose trusts, which can be useful in a variety of estate-planning exercises and commercial transactions; and employee trusts, often created as part of an employee share-ownership plan for the benefit of employees, their relatives and dependants.

Jersey provides a secure haven for the tax-free administration of offshore trusts, with many fiduciary services companies able to provide efficient and cost-effective services for the creation and management of trusts. The island has a long history of political stability, with its own independent government and laws, and freedom to implement its own tax regime. These features, combined with a strong economy and full employment, inspire confidence for its future and continued status as a leading international finance centre.

The Centurion Group's head office, in Beresford Street, St. Helier

Structured offshore wealth and business solutions

Centurion Trust Group is a privately owned independent trust house offering confidential, personal and professional offshore services to individual, corporate and institutional clients. Established in 1970, the group has developed into a strong multidisciplinary professional business.

The group provides clients with tailored solutions for their wealth and business management needs through structured financial arrangements and products, and the establishment and administration of offshore entities and businesses. It also has a diverse, worldwide and high-profile client base and has substantial client assets under management or administration.

Mainly based in St. Helier, Jersey, the group has associated operations in Mauritius, Barbados and Bermuda and seeks to conduct business outside of time-zone constraints. It is registered to carry on trust business with the Jersey Financial Services Commission and is one of the few remaining registered independent and privately owned trust houses in Jersey. The group aims to deliver professionalism, integrity and continuity of service, together with innovation, creativity and flexibility, in an increasingly highly regulated offshore market place.

The group provides a comprehensive range of services through its companies and affiliates, drawing on the collective professional backgrounds and experience of its dedicated team of individuals. Services are divided into four main areas: trust and company administration services, professional services, capital services, and commercial trading services.

Trust and company administration services include the establishment of trusts and partnerships and the incorporation of companies. Also included are the provision of registered and commercial office services, the provision of trustees and protectors for trusts, general partners and nominee limited partners for partnerships and directors, as well as secretaries and nominee shareholders for companies.

With regard to trust services, for example, trusts are created for a variety of reasons – among them investment holding, asset protection, confidentiality and international tax planning. Under the trust concept, individuals may divest themselves of legal ownership of assets whilst still preserving the assets for the benefit of themselves, their families or others under the terms provided for the trust deed. The trustee is the legal owner of the assets, the beneficiaries have a simultaneous equitable right. There is no statutory requirement for trust accounts to be audited or filed with local authorities.

Over the years, the group has been involved in the establishment of many trusts. It has also worked closely with an individual's other professional advisers, ensuring that the trust achieves the individual's desired tax planning, asset protection and succession objectives.

Professional services include accountancy services. Among them are the preparation and finalising of accounts to specified recognised accounting standards, taxation advice on offshore taxation issues and legal advice for group-managed entities and transaction structures.

The personal touch

For example, with regard to tax services, tax-saving schemes can be put to various types of use. These schemes should not be looked at in isolation, for the most suitable result can often be obtained by combining different strategies. The most appropriate arrangement mainly depends on the domicile and residence of a client or its business and the location of its assets and activities. Appropriate areas where tax planning can most commonly be effective include onshore investment by non-residents, non-residents working onshore but domiciled elsewhere, property development and investment, consultant and employee services, international trading and/or holding companies, and onshore investment with high capital tax charges. The group has put numerous such arrangements into place for its clients.

Capital services include portfolio valuation services

Directors James Hardcastle FCA and Michael Sun

Client Services Director, James Muir B. Eng (Hons) FCCA

(with access to Bloomberg market information feeds and other specialist fund and stock databases), stock and fund reports, corporate finance advisory services, funds administration and services for structured finance and capital markets special purpose vehicles. For instance, with regard to capital market services, special purpose vehicles can be established in an offshore location where it is desirable to isolate the purpose or transaction from the other activities of a party having an interest or proposed interest in the transaction, or where the transaction dictates that the vehicle should not be treated as controlled or owned by any party to that transaction. Uses of special purpose vehicles include securitisations, bond issues, debt/inventory defeasance, and off-balance sheet funding. The group has been involved in a number of such structures.

Commercial trading services include the provision of general offshore trading services to commercial organisations. These services include invoicing, arranging letters of credit and trade financing and organising delivery of shipments.

For example, with regard to trading services, international trading companies can be established to carry on a trade between two or more overseas locations. The invoicing company may alternatively act as a sales or purchasing agent, in return for a commission based on the turnover of goods or services which are supplied in one country but used in another. By establishing an invoicing company in an offshore location, it may be possible for funds to be accumulated which may not be subject to taxation. The group has established links with the international trading divisions of banks. It is also familiar with the use and negotiation of letters of credit on an international basis for these types of transactions and acts for a number of international trading companies.

Centurion Trust Group has a global network of long-established professional associations with investment advisers and banks, law firms and accountancy practices and other financial market professionals. It relies on this network to adopt, where possible, a jurisdictional 'neutral' approach, structuring and tailoring offshore wealth and management solutions in a way that provides a client with the most practicable and cost-effective offshore arrangement possible – whilst also taking into account both the client's offshore and onshore circumstances. In an ever-changing fiscal and regulatory environment, the group does not believe it should be tied to any one particular jurisdiction. Instead, it prefers to straddle jurisdictions in order to achieve, as far as possible, flexibility and security for the client's preferred wealth and business structure.

The group is firmly committed to understanding the client's requirements and working with the client and the client's other professional advisers to achieve the desired wealth and business management solution. The goal is to ensure that any new structure will complement the established framework of the financial affairs of the client and his or her business affairs, taking into account residence and domicile, commercial purposes, anonymity, principal objects, political stability in jurisdictions of choice, switching, and exchange control.

To improve the quality of its client services, the group is firmly committed to the development and use of information technology. Over recent years, with in-house programmers, it has developed its own i:face global trust administration system. It also has developed investment portfolio monitoring software for trustees and fiduciaries, and an Internet-based interface system with an independent third party, isentry, to act as a gatekeeper and enable clients to access information online held by Centurion without potentially adverse tax consequences.

The objective is to provide a virtual offshore environment for clients. Through this environment, the client's offshore affairs can be seamlessly administered, with optimum client transparency and confidentiality, but without compromising the trusted personal relationship service Centurion has established over the years.

The Centurion Trust Group is one of the leading independent private trust houses in the offshore industry. As such, it is firmly placed to provide clients with a flexible, comprehensive, and high standard of professional services in the years ahead in order to achieve their short-term or long-term wealth and business management objectives.

Administration Centre

75

The trust specialist

Specialist in fiduciary services

Volaw Trust & Corporate Services Limited is one of Jersey's leading independent fiduciary services companies. Established in 1982, it specialises in the formation and management of trusts, companies and other fiduciary vehicles and structures, whether created in Jersey or other jurisdictions.

The business operates from modern premises in St. Helier's central business district. It employs some 50 professional staff, with a variety of qualifications and backgrounds including law, accountancy, taxation, banking, investment management and company secretarial. It is responsible for the administration of over 1,400 trusts, companies and partnerships that together hold assets worth in excess of US$5,000 million.

Volaw Trust Company is closely associated with the legal practice of Voisin & Co., one of Jersey's longest established commercial law firms. Voisin & Co. is able to offer expert legal advice on the creation and use of the entities that Volaw manages. To advise companies and individual clients on how best to establish offshore fiduciary structures for tax planning, estate planning and other financial planning purposes, the company cooperates with a worldwide network of professional advisers. This network can also be tapped to offer clients a broad range of financial and legal expertise. The company is a member of the Eu-Lex International Practice Group and the Professional Fiduciary Group, both of which provide a business network with stringent standards to ensure that clients referred between members receive high-quality service.

Considerable effort is devoted to understanding and anticipating clients' financial needs and then helping them to establish practical and effective solutions that meet those needs. The firm places great emphasis on providing a professional, high-quality service in a timely and efficient manner. It also strives to develop and maintain excellent working relationships with its clients, combining a responsive, flexible team approach with personal service, creative thinking and an international outlook.

Most of Volaw's clients fall into one of five areas of business, with teams of experienced staff specialising in each of these areas. Institutional, expert and sophisticated investors often turn to collective investment funds, which are generally unique and innovative specialist funds. Volaw can administer these, as well as special purpose vehicles, which are entities established to undertake one specific transaction – most commonly the purchase or financing of an asset or class of assets. The firm's expertise has been demonstrated in many ground-breaking transactions in this field.

Other popular products include offshore employee benefit schemes, which are structures designed to provide tax-neutral benefit planning for individuals employed by corporations, and structures for corporate clients. The latter are called on for financing, balance sheet management or tax planning reasons.

However, the company's core business remains wealth management for private clients. This involves assisting high net-worth individuals in estate planning and protecting their wealth via the creation of trusts and other entities. In this area, its services are similar to those of traditional private bankers, but without the conflicts of interest that often arise with private banking.

Volaw is committed to continual development and improvement of its information and communications technology systems, allowing it to provide an efficient service and more effective reporting to clients. This ongoing programme, coupled with a modern and innovative approach to meeting clients' needs, keeps the company at the forefront of Jersey's financial services industry.

The personal approach

Volaw Trust Company, Don Road, St. Helier

Broad-based expertise

Moore Stephens in Jersey is part of Moore Stephens Europe Limited, with member firms in more than 40 countries, from Iceland in the west to the Ukraine in the east, and Morocco in the south to Norway in the north. Moore Stephens Europe is under the umbrella of Moore Stephens International Limited, one of the world's top 20 accounting and consulting networks, which has some 11,000 staff based in 380 offices in 80 countries strategically located around the world.

The company established an office in Jersey in 1970, in association with a local accounting firm, to primarily service the requirements of a small number of Moore Stephens clients located in the island. There was a small audit facility, together with a trust and company administration presence. At that time virtually all of the company's offshore work was structured elsewhere, but emphasis switched to the island as the Moore Stephens Jersey office developed.

In November 1974, Moore Stephens Jersey separated from its original associates and Clive Barton, who was trained in Moore Stephens London, was appointed as Audit Manager. He became a Partner in 1976 and Senior Partner two years later. Since then, the firm has grown and developed into one of the largest trust, accountancy and consultancy companies in the island.

Moore Stephens Jersey is part of the offshore group of offices, which includes Guernsey, Isle of Man and Gibraltar. The firm offers an extensive range of services, including the establishment of international structures and taxation advice, trust and company administration, consultancy and forensic accounting, and protection of family wealth. All of these services are designed to meet the needs of an internationally diverse client base. This encompasses corporate and private clients with varied business and personal requirements, including international property ownership and development, wealth management, shipping, airlines, fashion, retail, sports and the media.

First Island House, head office of Moore Stephens Offshore Group, situated in the business district of St. Helier

What sets Moore Stephens apart from other providers in the island is the general character of the firm and the manner in which the Partners and staff deliver these services. While professional expertise is fundamental, there is a real warmth in the relationship between this firm's staff and its clients, whether long-standing or newly estab-

Welcome to Moore Stephens!

lished. Accessibility to all the Partners is a mantra rather than a mission statement.

Moore Stephens is totally committed to the maintenance and development of the highest standards in Jersey's finance industry. Its well-trained staff are, if possible, recruited locally and the 80 Partners and staff are heavily involved in the fabric of island life, including local government, education, the arts, youth and business ventures, charities and sports.

Audit Floor

The Museum and Gallery situated on New North Quay

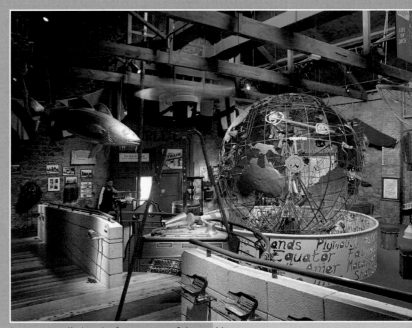
Jerseymen sailed to the four corners of the world

The People Gallery

Jersey's maritime past

Maritime Museum and Occupation Tapestry Gallery

The Occupation Tapestry, completed to mark the 50th anniversary of the island's liberation

Memorial to the victims of German oppression

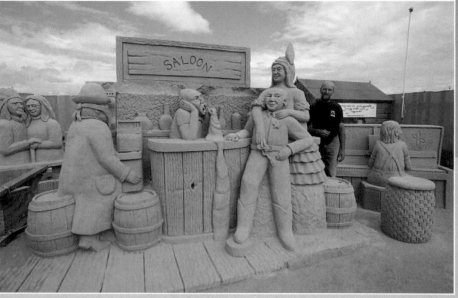

Sand sculpture

St. Helier

Ariadne steam clock

The Dolphin statue and fountain

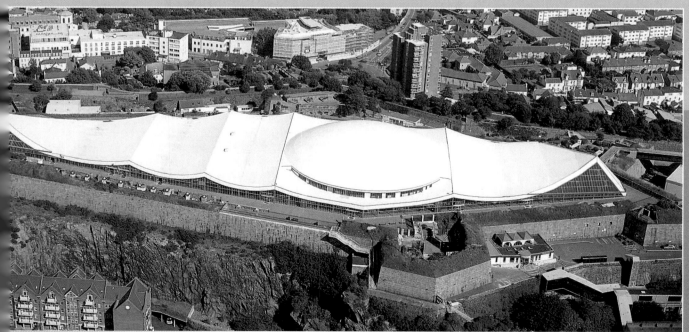

Fort Regent Leisure Centre

Island Fortress Occupation Museum

Elizabeth Marina

Sailing with style

The magnificent Sunseeker

Harbour & Marinas

Sons of the sea

The harbour entrance

Unloading containers

Modern ferries link the island with Europe and the UK

St. Helier Marina, New North Pier and Old Harbour

Boating, a Jersey tradition

First-class communications

A fast, reliable postal service

Jersey Fund Managers have more than £100 billion under management

Economy

a continuing success story

For an island of some 45 square miles (116 sq. km) with few natural resources, Jersey has maintained a remarkably prosperous economy over several centuries – often outdoing its nearest neighbours in the United Kingdom and France. Today it boasts a gross national income of around 2 billion pounds (source: Oxera), generated mainly over the last 40 years by revenue from financial services and tourism.

Jersey's economic success underlines the hard work, determination and imagination of its people to make the most of their assets. One of its biggest problems, though, is accommodating a rapidly growing population – as businesses import manpower to sustain an expanding economy.

As a Crown dependency loyal to the UK monarchy for 800 years, Jersey has generally looked north to England for its trading links. These were based on a succession of dominant industries. In the 17th century, for instance, the economy depended greatly on the knitting of socks and 'jerseys'. This lucrative occupation eventually attracted too many local workers, obliging the authorities to pass a law ensuring the men also tended the fields.

Two centuries later, cider-apple orchards sprang up all over the island. This agricultural boom was then replaced by one in shipbuilding in the mid-19th century. Other agricultural exports later grew in importance and contributed to the island's prosperity. They included the famous Jersey cow and the Jersey Royal potato – which is still its most important export crop, accounting for over two-thirds of agricultural turnover.

After World War Two, tourism became the dominant industry. As faster air and sea travel opened up Jersey to Europeans, the British in particular fell for the island's many charms and made it a priority summer holiday destination. Tourist numbers have undoubtedly declined over recent decades, a trend exacerbated by the development of cheaper package holidays to sunnier climes. Yet the island – together with a highly developed accommodation infrastructure comprising hotels, guesthouses, campsites, holiday villages and self-catering apartments – still attracts close to a million visitors annually and derives around 6% of its annual income from tourism.

Luckily for Jersey, the expansion of its financial services industry has more than compensated for tourism's gradual decline. Financial services – a broad sector that includes banks, as well as various investment, trust and fund companies – today contribute to around 60% of the island's GDP and provide employment for more than one in five of the workforce.

There are no signs of a downturn in this industry, but its leaders and the authorities are well aware of its vulnerability to outside pressures and understand the potential dangers of over-reliance on one economic activity. The island's government has so far come up with few practical measures to promote more economic diversity. But there is an agreed policy to promote a more balanced economy.

Other important contributors to GDP, according to Oxford Economic Research Associates Limited, are the services sector (17% of the total), government services (8%), the construction industry (7%), manufacturing (2%), and agriculture and fisheries (1%). While agriculture contributes less than before to the local economy, those involved in this industry (together with horticulture) still make use of more than half the island's land for their activities. As in other sectors, relatively small but innovative businesses have made their mark here. Live cattle exports, for example, have increased recently thanks to demand from UK farmers replenishing their herds.

In many respects, government action has lagged behind that of island businesses. Part of the island's success stems from the willingness of Jersey entrepreneurs to exploit new markets and fill niches in existing ones. They have benefited from a well-educated workforce and, although it is hard to compete for labour with the all-powerful finance sector, not every islander wants to work in financial services. Hence the numerous very small businesses, many of which provide innovative services and products. The island has a population of around 87,000 people, yet it is home to some 4,200 firms, with some two-thirds of them employing five staff or less.

More and more people are employed in information and communication technologies – an industry expected to grow significantly. The sector is already an important economic activity in Jersey, servicing the finance sector and ensuring that it benefits from the latest technological developments.

The hope now is that the ICT sector will grow in its own right, serving new clients.

Despite stiff competition from abroad, Jersey is having considerable success in developing this fourth pillar of the economy to support finance, tourism and agriculture. The largest offshore IT services group, for example, has offices in Jersey, Guernsey and the Isle of Man and more than 600 clients for its software, facilities management and Internet hosting services

Datacentres, used for e-commerce, represent another growth area. The biggest is Foreshore, located in a former electricity generating hall, adjacent to stand-by generators. Although Jersey experiences very few power cuts, these back-up facilities provide additional comfort for e-commerce service providers. The company operates one of the world's first offshore, neutral Internet Business Exchanges to be independent of any telecoms operator or Internet Services Provider. It currently manages servers for parent companies from Europe, the US, South Africa and the Middle East; they are involved in a range of activities, including financial services, publishing, broking, retail and software.

Further growth is expected in the management and distribution of intellectual property. This is an area where Jersey can maximise its existing expertise in financial services and the law, as well as its low taxation and first-class infrastructure.

The ICT sector should receive a boost from the opening up of the telecommunications sector and the introduction of competition to the former monopoly operated by the government-owned Jersey Telecom. The company plans to spend £80 million over five years on new capital projects aimed at keeping the island at the forefront of telecoms services. It was also one of the world leaders in the

deployment of high-speed Internet services using ADSL technology. Competitors are emerging in the telecoms arena, some of which already provide a range of voice, data and Internet services – albeit mainly to the finance sector. At least one is planning to compete directly with Jersey Telecom in many areas. The Channel Islands telecoms market, valued at £184 million in 1999, is expected to grow to around £300 million over the next few years.

The local electricity supplier, the Jersey Electricity Company, has built a high-speed fibre-optic cable running alongside one of its undersea electricity cables linking Jersey, Guernsey, the UK and France. The cable doubles the island's telecoms capacity with the outside world, as well as increasing choice and the resilience of the local telecoms network.

PayOffshore.Com, which is partly owned by Jersey Telecom, claims to have been the first complete offshore Internet e-commerce solutions provider in Europe. Its network infrastructure is located across two buildings in Jersey, joined by a high-speed fibre link with two IP connections to the Internet. This provides a secure environment for hosting e-commerce services, including financial transactions online through leading financial institutions.

The growth in ICT has benefited other businesses providing alternative sources of revenue.

The Indigo Lighthouse Group, for example, is a Scottish-owned company which has established its European distribution centre in Jersey. This new centre supplies two million pairs of contact lenses a year to customers all over Europe.

The Jersey postal system's efficiency also contributes significantly to the success of the locally based Flying Brands Group. This group includes Flying Flowers, Britain's largest flowers-by-post company. It despatches more than £13 million worth of flowers each year, many of them grown in the company's own glasshouses in Jersey.

Jersey Post itself is developing new sources of income, including a sophisticated direct mail and fulfilment service called ProMail. High-performance printing and enclosure equipment is used to print and mail millions of bank statements, regular bills and other secure documents.

Innovators in the world of e-commerce

Other local companies have succeeded in expanding their markets outside of the island and now make a useful contribution to its exports. Many relatively small companies provide a range of innovative products and services, and the island's government has acknowledged the importance of this sector of the economy for producing more diversity.

To develop new industries and enterprises, the government recently established an Emerging Industries Board. It believes, for instance, that there is considerable scope for the development of a local film industry. A grant to a Jersey-born producer recently resulted in The Crooked Mile, a critically acclaimed feature film partly shot in the island . A Film Fund with an associated Screen Commission are also being set up, in order to create a platform for further film successes. Analysts estimate that this move, involving an investment of £2 million over three years, will produce direct and indirect returns of over £3.5 million.

The St. Helier harbours are busy all year round. Well over half a million tonnes of goods pass through the port annually, in addition to some 450,000 passengers arriving mainly from the UK and France. Jersey has some 5,000 registered craft and receives more than 6,500 yacht visits a year. Not surprisingly, the island has a thriving marine services industry, although to date this has been used almost exclusively by local and visiting boat-owners. However, with the expansion of marina facilities, especially in St. Helier, the island is increasingly perceived as a good location for UK boat-owners to base their craft.

Considerable investment opportunities await outsiders. Commercial property in Jersey is proving to be a good investment for institutional investors, with prices and yields approaching London levels. The construction industry continues to boom, as the finance sector keeps on expanding. This is evidenced by the recent building of a brand new headquarters for Standard

A vibrant retail sector

A world leader in financial services

Modern airport facilities

A well-motivated workforce

Chartered Grindlays, among other banks here. That said, manpower shortages still hamper construction companies – which explains why some major projects are being undertaken as joint ventures with other local or French and UK firms. The vast development on the St. Helier Waterfront is a good example: part of it is a joint venture between a local construction group and a French company. Intended to create Europe's finest waterfront complex, the project has attracted considerable interest from outside investors. A leisure complex containing eight separate leisure and retail units is under construction. This provides the island with a ten-screen multiplex cinema, a nightclub, several restaurants, a health club, and an Aquatic Centre featuring a 25-metre pool, flume rides and a wave pool. The complex, plus a new luxury hotel to be built nearby, will prove a shot in the arm for the local economy and the tourism industry in particular.

Traditional leisure tourism continues to face tough competition from foreign destinations. But Jersey hopes to benefit from the tremendous growth in business tourism, including conferences, business meetings, incentive travel and corporate hospitality. The Jersey Conference Bureau already helps to generate significant conference business, which represents some 50,000 hotel bednights a year. Several specialist organisations provide facilities and activities for conference delegates, ranging from paintball shooting to tall-ship sailing. Venues used by conference organisers include the recently restored century-old Jersey Opera House, Fort Regent – the Napoleonic fortress converted into a leisure complex, and several large hotels including the island's biggest, the Hotel de France.

Jersey's retail businesses also contribute to the general economy. Many specialise in selling a wide range of jewellery, watches and perfumes.

A benign system of taxation also draws wealthy individuals to the island to buy property. Their number is strictly limited on an annual quota basis and they have to buy properties which are out of the reach of most islanders, which means they have to pay £1 million plus to be allowed in. These individuals also have to make a significant contribution to the island's exchequer. Among those who have made their home in Jersey are David Crossland, the founder of travel giant MyTravel (formerly Airtours), TV personality Alan Whicker, author Jack Higgins, golfer Ian Woosnam and former Formula One world champion Nigel Mansell.

The States of Jersey are keen to support and encourage new businesses. But unlike most other jurisdictions, they do not offer any subsidised start-up schemes or financial incentives. This is partly because the aim of such schemes is to attract new jobs, whereas Jersey already has full employment and, if anything, the economy suffers from overheating. Attracting more businesses will only add to the pressure on scarce resources, particularly manpower. However, the States are committed to promoting a more diversified economy, to complement the long-standing successes of financial services and tourism.

A thriving construction sector

Ronez granite quarry

...ular tourist destination

...ficient port infrastructure

The Jersey Royal, an export winner

Delivering quality through technology

Telephone service was first established in Jersey in 1895 by the National Telephone Company. Taken over by the Post Office in 1912 and then the States of Jersey in 1923, the island's telecommunications systems have continued to be developed and are on a par with those of the most advanced countries in the Western World.

Jersey Telecom has made significant investments over the last decade to provide the island with a modern, high-quality telecommunications network and plans to spend an average of £14 million a year up to 2007.

The island's telecommunications network is extremely modern and uses the latest technologies.

The fully digital exchange network is upgraded on a regular basis to ensure Jersey remains at the cutting edge in terms of standards and new services. Digital connections reach out to customers' premises via an extensive fibre optic network, over which connections to the System X exchanges are made, or sophisticated Local Area Network (LAN) connections provided. Up-to-the-minute Synchronous Digital Hierarchy (SDH) systems provide the backbone for the inter-exchange connections and the submarine cables which link the island with the outside world. A new microwave link between Jersey and France has also recently been installed, to provide increased capacity, resilience

and access to diverse feeds for the company's Internet backbone service. External links between the island and the UK, Guernsey and France have been established via a combination of submarine cables and microwave systems. Heavy investment has been made in ensuring there is sufficient capacity within the external network to cater for the failure of any single route, as well as allowing for future growth and development. Quality, availability and reliability are key words in the provision of any telecoms services. That is especially so on Jersey, whose economy depends on meeting the special telecoms requirements of its first-class finance centre. Jersey Telecom's policy is to provide security, resilience and protection of the networks and services through diversification of routes and/or duplication of equipment. Work was recently completed on the Network Operations Centre (NOC), a state-of-the-art network management facility. It represents a significant investment and is a key part of the company's strategy for continued success. The centre has brought together over 40 network staff that previously worked at many different sites across the island.

The NOC is a unique offering, allowing the company to monitor all aspects of its network from a single location that has a total and real-time view of its own network, enabling it to immediately identify how one part may be impacting on another. Complex technology, by its very

A General Packet Radio Service (GPRS) will soon be available in Jersey, connecting local mobile phone customers to the Internet and improving data transfer speeds. In line with some other mobile operators in the UK, a full GPRS network was recently installed. This network offers an 'always on' high-capacity service, bringing Internet content such as colour web browsing, e-mail on the move, powerful visual communications and multimedia messages to suitable mobile devices. Customers will be able to download Internet pages at similar speeds to a wireline connection. Importantly for businesses, GPRS can also offer a secure wireless link to their own corporate intranets: access to files, e-mail and diaries will therefore be available to users whilst on the move.

The mobile services network now supports over 70% of local users, 70% of the population and connects with more than 125 other foreign networks. The mobile network supports mobile fax and data services, as well as Short Messaging Service (text messaging) and a pre-paid mobile service. In addition to standard telephony, all major services such as ISDN, Centrex, Digital Private Circuits, Telex, Fax & Data, Voicemail and Paging are also available to the island community.

The firm provides a number of Internet services to the island, which connect to the Internet Backbone Service, a fully resilient high-grade connection to the World Wide Web. JustConnect is a 'pay as you go' Internet access service, whilst the jerseyinsight.com portal offers extensive and useful information about Jersey as well as the latest local, national and international news. Jerseyinsight.com will also become the delivery mechanism for future interactive broadband content and information services.

Jersey Telecom was one of the first European networks to provide residential ADSL (Asynchronous Digital Subscriber Line) technology direct for island homes to enjoy 'always on' high-speed connection to the Internet at a fixed charge. Geographic coverage across Jersey is 99.9% and local penetration is one of the highest in Europe.

The company is also a leading supplier of all types of customer premises equipment, networks and structured data wiring systems and offers a range of fully managed telecommunications solutions. It has achieved Cisco Premier Partner status and also has become Prestige Partners for Systimax Structured Connectivity Solutions, becoming one of only 11 companies in the UK to achieve this status.

Value for money is also extremely important in terms of sustaining economic activity and encouraging future growth. In a small island such as Jersey, it is well known that there are many additional costs which have to be taken into account when connecting with the outside world and that the local marketplace is very small in terms of providing economies of scale. Nevertheless, the price of the total package for telecommunications services in Jersey compares favourably and is competitive with the UK and other European countries.

Prices for long-distance calls have fallen dramatically over the past few years as new technologies, lower costs and competition have all taken effect and this downward trend is set to continue. Despite these reductions, local call rates remain extremely low and rentals are competitive with UK rates. It is essential for Jersey's economy that the trend towards lower prices in the long-distance call markets is maintained and the company is committed to ensuring that this is the case. It is also vital that a balance is struck between lowering these prices and maintaining a low-cost local tariff structure which benefits small businesses and

nature, will at some point fail and thus it is an integral role of the NOC to ensure that this risk of failure and any effect on customer service is minimised. Ultimately the NOC represents an investment centred on maintaining the quality of Jersey Telecom's networks to the highest possible standards.

The company has comprehensive support agreements with its major suppliers, ensuring 24/7 technical support, and has extended these arrangements so that they proactively monitor and maintain the company's fixed network exchanges outside of normal working hours. Furthermore, there are extensive disaster-recovery plans in place, covering all major failure situations. In the unlikely event of a total failure of one its fixed network buildings, the company has contracts with its key suppliers to guarantee the delivery of containerised replacement exchange equipment to Jersey within 24 hours.

the island community as a whole. The company recognises the importance of first-class telecommunications to the island's economy, and in particular the needs of the finance industry, which is heavily reliant on efficient, fast, cost-effective and manpower-saving telecommunications. It is also the company's policy to introduce new services and equipment as the need arises and to provide the telecommunication services for its customers to the highest standards of quality, on time and at a competitive price.

As a Jersey-based company for the people of Jersey, the company strives to grow its business. It values the strong links with its customers and the traditions built from being the established provider of telecommunications services in the island and remains firmly committed to providing modern and reliable communications solutions and excellent customer service.

Jersey Telecom intends to continue its excellent record of delivering value-for-money, world-class services and hopes to work efficiently and pragmatically with all industry players and stakeholders to develop a truly effective telecommunications market.

Delivering customer solutions

A mainstay of the island's economy and social structure for many decades, Jersey Post is one of the world's leading small postal authorities. As the main conduit for letters, packets and parcels locally and internationally, the company processes and delivers more than 70 million items locally, including despatches to the UK, along with some three million direct marketing leaflets. It is also an innovative and profitable business, thanks to an ongoing programme of new products and services. Since becoming independent of the British Post Office in 1969, the States of Jersey Committee for Postal Administration has provided regular postal services in keeping with its universal service duties. A big shake-up came in 1995, following a complete organisational review. The new focus on meeting customers' growing requirements, rather than just their basic needs, has led to something of a revolution at what is now known as Jersey

Post. Today the company – which is headquartered in modern purpose-built premises in St. Saviour – often receives delegations from sister organisations abroad eager to learn how to propel postal authorities into the 21st century.

Significant recent investment in both people and technology, not to mention a period of restructuring and repositioning, is paying dividends for the company and its customers. What is more, the company now has a vision of where and what it wants to be, including its desire to be a "chosen provider of customers' global distribution and communication solutions". As a result, profits continue to rise, regular customers are offered better products and services, and new customers are turning to the company as a reliable and efficient outsourcing partner.

Both the physical and electronic mail environments have benefited from initiatives. In the former, for example, improved management as well as new automation and information systems have driven up efficiency and quality. The small yet highly motivated staff is therefore able to process and deliver more mail than ever. Recent annual figures speak volumes. Some 90 vehicles on the island, not including bicycles, covered almost 700,000 miles to deliver forty percent more mail than five years before. That's not bad for a company of only 400 employees.

Yet the greatest changes have come in the electronic mail environment. Working through strategic partnerships and alliances, among them US-based Pitney Bowes – a leading provider of integrated mail and document management solutions, Jersey Post has introduced a raft of new products. These include mailing house services, hybrid mail support, and database and address field management services. More recently, the company has launched e-commerce and e-business support services, which are becoming popular with local customers and enterprises.

ProMail, the first of the new services, acts as a mailing house in tandem with Mailroom Services. A boon to the many island firms involved in finance, trust and fund administration and who need sophisticated mailing outsourcing facilities, ProMail provides address database management, printing and enveloping services. As an Automated Document Factory, it can print, envelope and mail reports and accounts, regular statements and invoices on behalf of customers large or small, locally based or in other offshore markets.

The very latest integrated solutions, targeted at all sectors of the business and residential markets, increasingly focus on meeting customer needs. The one-stop solution for both communication and distribution is now a reality for physical, retail, electronic mail, online commerce and hybrid mail channels, as Jersey Post continues to develop its unique Multi-Channel offering.

By way of example, highly automated envelopers and printers were used in a successful pilot scheme heralding the company's entry into the world of Electronic Bill Presentation and Payment (EBPP). Under the scheme, in one of the island's parishes, customers are able to view online and pay their local rates bill. The same programme is likely to be rolled out across the island. The company sees great potential for EBPP services – anywhere where large volumes of documents are in transit – in other offshore markets, including government, private sector, as well as business-to-business and business-to-consumer.

Further delivery solutions, likely to be launched by the company's ProMail business, are under consideration. The goal will be to reduce delivery

times, improve integrity, lower costs and create a full audit trail of customers' documents. Mailing house and e-business services are expected to grow dramatically for the company over the next few years. And as Internet purchases become increasingly popular, many companies on the island are turning to Jersey Post and its new businesses for fulfilment of e-commerce orders.

There has even been change within the Jersey Philatelic Department, which has responsibility for a wide range of products and services. Besides issuing definitive stamps, the department releases some ten sets of commemorative stamps annually, some commissioned from leading local artists. Prized by enthusiastic collectors worldwide, these stamps feature a variety of subjects, including major events, royalty, nature, transport and technology – often with a flavour or history specific to the island. Other products include Year Books, First-Day Cover

envelopes and Presentation Packs, as well as dedicated albums in which to keep them all. In a European postal first, the department has even issued an exclusive stamp incorporating 22-carat gold, the £10 Millennium Gold, a design that proved a huge hit with philatelists in and beyond the island.

Underlining island-wide confidence in Jersey Post, around twenty percent of the population has already signed up to the company's free email service. Customers of every kind, it seems, are sold on the idea of their new and very forward-looking postal authority.

Jersey Electricity Company headquarters

The Jersey Electricity Company has played a major role in island life since its formation in 1924 and today still remains one of the island's largest employers and providers of services.

Demand for electricity has grown over the years in line with the island's infrastructure – both residential and commercial. As the current sole supplier, Jersey Electricity has made significant investment and looked at many innovative ways to ensure that the whole island's demand for power is met at the most economic cost, taking into consideration the need to ensure security of supply. In addition the company has also placed itself at the forefront of technical excellence in building services design, to ensure energy efficiency at point of use as well as at point of production.

The most recent of these projects is the Channel Islands Electricity Grid, completed at the end of 2000, bringing immediate benefits to customers by substantially reducing dependence on fuel oil for electricity production. The grid comprises an interconnector placed on the seabed which links both Jersey and Guernsey to mainland Europe, giving Jersey Electricity Company the freedom to exploit for its customers emerging competition in the European electricity market. The fibre optics in the continental powerlinks also promise competitive choice in the future for telecoms users. This is the second link from Europe to Jersey, the first having been completed in 1985.

In addition to the investment in the £50 million Channel Islands Electricity Grid, Jersey Electricity continues to invest in its plant at La Collette Power Station to ensure that it can independently meet

State-of-the-art control room at La Collette power station

the whole island's demand for power in addition to providing important emergency standby and a deep winter top-up service. Strategic security and overall reliability are paramount to the island's finance industry and Jersey Electricity is proud of its record of security of supply being amongst the highest in the world. Equally importantly, the cessation of bulk energy production at La Collette is a major factor in Jersey meeting its obligations

under International Climate Change Treaties to reduce CO2 emissions.

Today there is an increasing awareness of the effects of energy use. People are asking more about the impact on both the local and global environment. It is the company's belief that the responsibility for limiting that impact is shared between those who supply energy and those who use it. A responsible balance is sought between the costs

Tourism

By Robert Parker,
Chairman,
Hotel de France

A blueprint for success

Beautiful sandy beaches

Alfresco dining

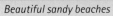

Historic La Hougue Bie

The world-renowned Eric Young Orchid Foundation

Friendly bars abound

To understand the challenges of the future, knowledge of the past is crucial. For Jersey the comfort of past successes and the fear of change probably represent the major stumbling blocks to realising the island's future potential.

Tourism in Jersey started seriously expanding in the 1950s, reaching its peak in the 1980s. The island had a number of unique selling points. It was considered an exotic destination for the UK mass market, with low taxes on drink and cigarettes making prices very attractive. Eating out was very reasonable and the quality of the "Jersey product" was considerably superior to most Mediterranean resorts. In those days, flying to what we now consider exotic destinations, such as the Caribbean, was fabulously expensive.

So what has happened in the intervening years? The quality of most Mediterranean resorts has improved considerably. Long-haul travel is now relatively inexpensive and good staff cost around twenty times more in Europe than those in many

long-haul destinations. So the cost of a holiday in Europe is comparable in price with its long-haul counterpart.

Jersey has also developed a very successful finance industry, which has taken over as the island's foremost industry. As a result there has not been the same commitment to tourism as for many of our competitors, for whom tourism is their economic lifeblood. On the other hand, the island has developed an excellent selection of fine restaurants, a number of golf courses, sophisticated shopping and a business infrastructure that supports a growing conference market.

Today Jersey still has its considerable natural beauty, thanks to strict planning laws, and many world-class historical sites which are attractive to the more discerning visitor. But it no longer has the considerable cost benefits of the past. Nor does

The quiet of the countryside

it now have a position in the market which ensured most hotels were nearly fully booked for the season during the first few months of the year. In the current economic climate, a tourist industry will always exist here – based on the island's natural beauty and unique character. But tourism will not provide a serious second pillar for the island's economy, unless we can grow it by properly investing in developing markets.

So what could the future hold? There is an exciting project to develop part of Fort Regent into a conference hall, with a seating capacity of 2,500. This hall would have direct access to the Fort's battlements and offer stunning views over Elizabeth Castle and St. Aubin's Bay. The development would more than likely pay for itself, substantially benefiting the local economy by bringing in more large conferences. Moreover, the island would attract world-class events –many linked to Jersey's status as an international financial centre – seeking a photogenic venue. This project provides an opportunity to develop an event-led tourism strategy, thus creating massive media exposure and helping to promote out-of-season bookings and an expanding short-break market.

In order to maximise the short-break market's potential, I believe Jersey also needs the introduction of low-cost airlines. Those who plan ahead can already obtain very reasonably priced flights to and from the island. But the perception in the market place is that many people determine their short-break destinations on the basis of where the low-cost airlines fly. I believe the power of this perception as a marketing tool is totally out of sync with the reality of the numbers. However, this idea

The family island

Honeymoon island

Jersey Zoo

The 13th-century magnificence of Mont Orgueil Castle

Picturesque fishing villages

achieves front-of-mind status for a resort – far in excess of what a considerable advertising campaign would achieve. The low-cost carrier Ryanair is presently very keen to fly to Jersey. I hope by the time you read this that the island authorities have negotiated sensibly with this airline, or any similar one, and that another opportunity is in place to expand our tourism market for all.

Being an island, we can set up an island-wide intranet which would act as a quick and easy information provider for

A choice of six golf courses

St. Helier, a shopaholics' dream

places of interest, what to do and a booking service. In a relatively small market, some activities providers find it difficult to exist because of the high overheads. A good example is operating a booking service for a fishing charter boat. An intranet would open the way for more specialised activities to become economically viable, offering a wider choice to our visitors. Local clubs and associations could then effectively promote their

events, improving the already significant benefit that cultural exchange brings for both locals and visitors. Jersey is a permanent community where the locals far outnumber the visitors. The island therefore has a depth of character that is impossible to achieve in a seasonal purpose-built resort. It is not surprising, then, that return visits are high. We currently have some excellent events. On the sporting side, for example, there is the international under-21 football competition with teams such as Manchester United. The newly refurbished Opera House also hosts some superb cultural events. Unfortunately these events are not given the promotional support they deserve: standard generic advertising is of little benefit unless it is balanced with detailed product offerings.

Jersey has many of the basic ingredients to create an exciting world-class resort, but we need to grab the opportunities that exist if we are to maximise our potential. It is possible, but we cannot keep protecting the past structure of our tourism product at the expense of the developing markets. The island could become a leading resort. Yet the biggest obstacle is the culture of many hoteliers and service providers, who are protecting their market position, and a government that is more interested in not upsetting any particular segment. We need to move forward with conviction, embracing the challenges of change without becoming sidelined by politics or individuals' self interest. In the end it is up to us. We can have a world-class tourism business... or the current decline will continue leaving only those who have invested for the future to survive.

Guardians of Elizabeth Castle

Jersey War Tunnels

Elegance & tradition

Dining at the Cristina Hotel

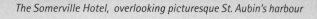

Set in superb locations around Jersey's south coast, the three establishments in the Dolan Hotels chain are among the island's finest. Each of these individually owned three-star hotels boasts a panoramic sea vista. They are also renowned for offering a first-class service, cuisine and comfort, in keeping with such unique and individual hotels. Dolan Hotels are perfect for both business and pleasure, with easy access to both the island's airport and its capital, St. Helier. Throughout the year, the hotels prove popular centres for both incentive and conference groups. Holidaymakers especially appreciate the beautiful situation: each establishment offers south-facing rooms, many with balconies, with idyllic views of the sea and beaches.

In the centre of St. Brelade's Bay, close to the beach, the Golden Sands Hotel vaunts many up-to-the-minute facilities. Sheltered by tree-covered cliffs, the bay's curving beach attracts families and watersports enthusiasts. Most bedrooms afford breathtaking sea views, while all rooms are comfortable and tastefully furnished. They come with a private bathroom, satellite television, direct-dial telephone and facilities for making hot drinks – just as in the other Dolan Hotels. The 'Superior Rooms' also include a personal safe. Here, as in the other establishments, fresh Jersey produce features prominently on the restaurant's extensive menu, complemented by a competitively priced wine list.

Hotel Cristina

A children's playroom, supervised at mealtimes, allows parents to dine in peace. Guests may also enjoy a drink in the welcoming cocktail bar, or simply relax in the lounge bar.

The Somerville Hotel sits on a hillside, with a fine panorama of the yachting harbour as well as the village of St. Aubin and the bay beyond. Guests have the choice of two contrasting beaches – the sandy expanse of St. Aubin's Bay and the sheltered cove of Belcroute Beach – just minutes away on foot. On offer are some 60 comfortable and tastefully furnished bedrooms, most enjoying spectacular sea views. Facilities include a cocktail bar, lounge, a heated freshwater swimming pool with a terrace, and a private car park. The Somerville treats diners to English and continental dishes, both traditional and imaginative, often calling on the best of local produce.

The Cristina Hotel is delightfully situated on a hillside, surrounded by colourful and well-maintained gardens and with fine views of St. Aubin's Bay. All 62 bedrooms are furnished to international standards and feature en-suite baths and showers.

The Somerville Hotel, overlooking picturesque St. Aubin's harbour

Overlooking the bay, Indigo's restaurant offers fresh island produce through its daily changing table d'hôte and seasonal à la carte menus. On sunny days, alfresco dining is available in the sun lounge or on the terrace. A heated pool, licensed bar and private car park round off this hotel's facilities.

Regular courtesy minibuses run from these hotels to St. Helier, St. Aubin's Bay as well as St. Brelade's Bay. Which is only what you would expect from a hotel chain committed to the highest levels of service, hospitality and comfort.

The Golden Sands Hotel

The lounge of Hotel Cristina

The acclaimed film "The Crooked Mile", made in Jersey

Artist Katy Brown

Performance of Carmen at the Domaine des Vaux

Young musician Julie Robinson

Artist and sculpture, Gerald Palmer

La Fête Nouormande

Artist Simon Tupper

St. Helier's Day pilgrimage to the hermitage

Liberation Day procession

Artist Ian Rolls with Clive Barton, Senior Partner of Moore Stephens

Art on wheels

"The Story Tellers" Alfresco Arts in Howard Davis Park

Knights in combat at Mont Orgueil Castle

Jersey Symphony Orchestra

Battle Of Flo

wers

The good food island

All the right ingredients are here. Jersey offers an abundance of eating establishments and plenty of talented chefs to make the best of fresh local produce. Whether catering to residents or visitors, the island has something to please everyone.

Local restaurants, some of which are famous beyond Jersey's shores, satisfy gourmets of every persuasion. Among the leading eateries are Longueville Manor, which holds a coveted Michelin star, Jersey Pottery's Garden Restaurant, the Atrium brasserie at Hotel de France, Suma's and the Zanzibar Beach Bistro.

Informal dining is common throughout the island, although some restaurants still encourage patrons to put on their best bib and tucker in the evening – a noble tradition that underlines the importance accorded to fine dining. Good food is available at an amazing variety of places. They range from humble cafes to ancient inns, from trendy wine bars to bistros, brasseries and restaurants serving everything from tasty home fare to gourmet meals.

The island's best cuisine is equally varied. Jersey Bean Crock, which includes beans and pork, is dubbed the national dish. However, local delicacies often make use of fresh produce caught from the seas around Jersey, such as mussels, scallops and oysters: all grow relatively quickly, helped by the island's tremendous tidal variations. The now rare ormer, a shellfish found only in local waters, is an occasional speciality cooked by locals, as is conger soup. Fish dishes – calling on sole, red mullet, sea bass and shrimp – grace the menus of the best restaurants, such as the Old Court House Inn and Green Island Restaurant. Canny entrepreneurs, it is worth noting, have harnessed some wartime fortifications to raise shellfish for local markets and restaurants.

Thanks to the island's mild climate and fertile soils, fresh produce is regularly harvested from the countryside, including quality Jersey Royal potatoes, tomatoes, peppers, cauliflowers and even kiwis, as well as annual herbs such as mint, thyme and basil. Diners may often enjoy this produce at local eating establishments several weeks before the rest of the UK.

Jersey is renowned too for its selection of restaurants serving internationally popular cuisine. Typical specialities from France, India, Italy and China, among other countries, can be found all over the island.

Some restaurants are located in charming places, ranging from centuries-old inns and cottages to rustic farms and windmills. While it is not hard to find a terrace with panoramic views of the sea, the best tables should be booked in advance.

The Jersey cream tea still has much to recommend it. Traditionally eaten in the late afternoon, it comprises a pot of piping hot tea and a tray laden with scones, jam, butter and the distinctively yellow clotted cream made from the milk of Jersey cows. A delicious, if rather calorific, meal that every visitor to the island should try at least once.

In honour of its gastronomic excellence, Jersey organises the International Food Festival every May. Local and celebrity chefs vie with one another to create culinary masterpieces or compete for the prize of being named the island's best establishment. This event is merely the icing on the cake for an island clearly dedicated to serving the freshest and finest fare.

Garden Restaurant, Jersey Pottery

Gastronomy

Jersey Food Festival

The ormer, a local Jersey delicacy

Green Island Restaurant

Gastronomic delight

Bon appetit!

Longueville Manor

The Atrium Brasserie, Hotel de France

Zanzibar Beach Bistro

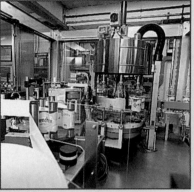

The bottling line at A.E. Smith & Son

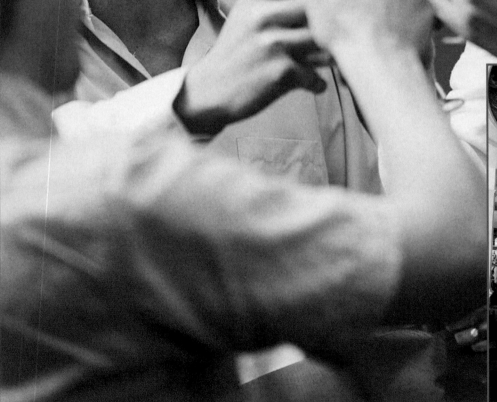

Relaxing with friends

The all-new S Bar

Ann Street Group, which employs more than 2,000 people, recently became part of the CI Traders Group, one of the few Channel Island companies with trading activities to be quoted on the London Stock Exchange. Ann Street's name derives from the location of its first brewery, set up in St. Helier some 130 years ago. Today it comprises a number of successful businesses in the Channel Islands, the UK and France. In addition to extensive interests in the brewing, bottling, manufacturing and sales of beers, wines, spirits and soft drinks, the group boasts a growing portfolio of hotels, restaurants and licensed premises.

Local beer-drinkers and many visitors enjoy the beverages produced by the Jersey Brewery, still situated in St. Helier, the capital of Jersey. The group's brewing division is the sole remaining commercial brewer on the island. Local draught beers are marketed under the Jersey Best and the award-winning Jersey Special labels. Its real ale operation, the Star and Tipsy Toad Brewery, is based in the historic village of St. Peter and produces traditional British-style cask-conditioned ales.

A range of national and local soft drinks are manufactured and distributed by A.E. Smith & Son, in St. Saviour, a subsidiary founded in 1894. Popular brands bottled include Pepsi Cola, Britvic, Irn Bru as well as the company's own range of drinks marketed under the name of Quencher.

The group's public house chain, in Jersey, includes some 57 managed and tenanted houses. It is the largest operation of its kind in the island. These licensed premises draw both local people and visitors, contributing significantly to the tourism sector. Embracing a variety of sizes and styles, many offer food while some also provide accommodation and entertainment. Fridays, in St. Helier, attracts a young crowd and even has conference facilities. Le Hocq, in St. Clement, is known for its gourmet restaurant, while the Cosmopolitan features a nightclub and bar.

Ann Street Freetraders, a recent entity, brings together the group's sales and wholesaling activities. The aim is to provide a consolidated distribution service to both the on- and off-licensed sectors, with leading international brands such as Carling and Grolsch. Wines, spirits, soft drinks and snack foods are also catered for.

Also in Jersey, Victor Hugo Wines, established in the early 1980s, is the group's wines and spirits arm and has several retail outlets on the island. It offers a wide range of international wines and spirits, among them Louis Latour burgundy, Laurent-Perrier champagne and Graham's Port, all carefully selected in line with current and emerging market trends. The very exclusive Victor Hugo Wine Club – limited to 70 members only – is also reputed for its regular dinners and tastings, hosted by wine specialists.

In Jersey the Group also has a wholesaling operation distributing tobacco products and a vending subsidiary offering cigarettes and a growing range of hot beverages and snack foods. In Guernsey, the group operates 29 managed and tenanted public houses in a similar style to Jersey. There is also a hotel division, the most prestigious property being the four-star St. Pierre Park Hotel: it has 135 bedrooms and is located in a 45-acre mature parkland site which incorporates a nine-hole golf course designed by the former British Open champion Tony Jacklin.

Fridays, a popular rendezvous for the young at heart

Ann Street, Jersey's only commercial brewer

Guernsey also operates an extensive wholesale drinks division under the name of Bucktrouts.

L'Abeille, the group's soft drinks company situated near Nantes in France, is the largest manufacturer of own label soft drinks in 1.5 PET bottles for major supermarket and hypermarket companies in that country.

In the UK, the group operates pubs and restaurants catering for all tastes. These include a well-established and expanding chain of licensed restaurants operating under the names of Blubeckers and Edwinns. Also popular and found in both town and country locations are Conquest Inns, which has some 60 tenancies.

From humble beginnings, the Ann Street Group has grown to become an integral part of Jersey's leisure and entertainment sector, while continuing to expand its successful businesses throughout the Channel Islands, the UK and France.

Victor Hugo Wines, the new retail outlet

Le Hocq Inn, situated in St. Clement's, famed for its gourmet food

Dannemarche Reservoir

The 18th-century Morel Farm

Coronation Park

Preserving the past

Centrally located, the parish of St. Lawrence stretches north from St. Aubin's Bay and shares borders with the parishes of St. Helier and St. Peter, as well as St. Mary's and St. John's. Besides the fine sandy beach, the major attractions here include the thought-provoking Jersey War Tunnels and the museum at Hamptonne.

Around a mile of St. Aubin's Bay lies within this parish, appealing to holidaymakers and water-sports enthusiasts. Whereas the north of the parish still has plenty of open agricultural land and once hosted china clay quarries, the southern coastline has witnessed much development in recent years.

St. Matthew's Glass Church at Millbrook was orig-inally built for people settling into the area in the 19th century. Years later, the widow of Sir Jesse Boot, founder of the retail chemists of the same name, turned this simple church into a place of great beauty by calling on the services of René Lalique. The French designer's Art Deco glasswork – including the font, altar rail, cross and pillars – are today considered to be amongst his greatest achievements. Beautiful Coronation Park, next door to the church, celebrates the coronation of King George VI and was also a gift from Lady Trent in memory of her husband.

A lack of fresh water in the late Victorian era spurred the government to create three new reser-voirs, all within this parish. Lined up north to south along Waterworks Valley, Handois, Dannemarche and Millbrook make a scenic route for walkers. A number of disused mills in the valley highlight the former importance of water power to the island's industries.

The Hamptonne Country Life Museum, south of Handois Reservoir, allows visitors to experience farming life on the island over the last three cen-turies. There are guided tours of the faithfully restored farm buildings (among them thatched

Parish of St. Lawrence

Millennium Stone

houses, a cider house, bakery, washhouse and stables) and meadows, as well as demonstrations of fast-disappearing rural skills. Other buildings of note here are the Langlois House, built in a French

Medieval style, and Hamptonne House, extended down the centuries and now restored to depict life in both the 1640s and 1730s. The parish boasts several traditional Jersey farms, including the 17th-century Morel Farm.

A unique heritage site is found in the heart of the parish, at the Jersey War Tunnels. In 1941 the island's World War Two occupiers intended the site – which lies some 40 metres below ground – to be an artillery barracks and store. The complex of tunnels and rooms, excavated mainly by forced and slave labour, was later converted into a hospital in

expectation of a British attack. But it was never used as such and today serves as the island's definitive Occupation museum, with an impressive exhibition on life in Jersey during that dark period.

Not far from here is the 11th-century parish church, which squats below a saddle-back tower. It also contains the island's oldest surviving bell. Close to the border with St. Mary's, Flying Flowers operates one of the island's most successful enterprises, delivering fresh flowers worldwide. A dynamic business that helps seal the good reputation of this charming parish.

Jersey War Tunnels

'Captive Island' at The German Underground Hospital

When the Germans departed Jersey in May 1945 after a five-year occupation, they left behind a vast array of defensive forts, walls and tunnels. One of the most impressive installations is the German Underground Hospital, located in the parish of St. Lawrence. Sensitively restored over the decades since the Second World War, the tunnels now house the island's definitive Occupation museum, a moving and permanent reminder of the island's most difficult period.

The Channel Islands' strategic position between France and Britain, and most crucially their status as "British soil", made them a highly prized possession for the German invaders arriving in July 1940. Determined to defend the Islands against any attempt to reclaim them, the occupiers turned the Islands into the most heavily defended part of the Atlantic Wall, a line of fortifications that eventually stretched from Norway to the Pyrenees.

On Jersey, the Germans launched their building programme in October 1941. Concrete and iron bunkers, towers, gun emplacements and sea walls were erected throughout the island. Tunnels were excavated to afford protection for the German forces from Allied air and sea attacks.
The Underground Hospital was originally planned as an artillery barracks and store and then in 1944 converted into a Casualty Clearing Station. It was the largest complex, with tunnels hewn 40

metres into a shale hillside. In the event of an Allied attack, it could have accommodated up to 500 casualties.

Like many of the defensive constructions in Jersey, this bomb-proof complex owes its existence to the toil of thousands of foreign workers. These labourers were shipped in from countries such as Russia, Poland, France and Spain by the Organisation Todt, which supplied labour wherever it was needed in the expanding Reich. Cruel working conditions and a starvation diet meant many men collapsed from exhaustion and disease. A poignant memorial to those who died – and "all who suffered hardship at that time" – is etched onto a wall plaque close to the tunnels' entrance. While the site's unassuming entrance may attract little more than a quick glance from today's visitors, few fail to marvel at the engineering feat accomplished here – and the human cost. The longest tunnels stretch for over a hundred metres. Several were unfinished and sealed up by the Germans. Another one collapsed, perhaps as a result of over-hasty construction.

As it turned out, the hospital facilities were never used. Abandoned after liberation in 1945, the complex became little more than a curiosity. In the 1960s, the island's authorities realised the importance of conserving traces of the German Occupation and the tunnels were turned into a museum.

In 2001 the museum received a major refit, dramatically enhancing the visitor experience. 'Captive Island', a new permanent exhibition, tells the story of the Occupation using the words and phrases of those who were actually there. The exhibition combines traditional and cutting-edge display techniques. Interactive exhibits, artefacts, photographs and film, documents and personal accounts now fill the wards – each one given over to a different chapter in this fascinating story. The tunnels are untouched: their unique chilling atmosphere remains. Captive Island throws light on the plight of everyone who spent time at this site and elsewhere on Jersey – whether islander, prisoner or German soldier.

Great care has been taken to preserve the core areas of the hospital. They include the operating theatre, fully equipped with historically accurate fixtures and fittings, and the cramped quarters set aside for medical staff. The original telephone

exchange and the head storeman's office remain, while the boiler room and air locks bear witness to some of the advanced heating and ventilation technology once installed here.

Visitors and tourists are well catered for, whatever their reason for coming. The Visitor Centre, refurbished at the end of 2002, has extensive parking and comprises a café and gift shop – both of which have full disabled access. Beautiful surroundings and a Garden of Reflection contribute to the sense of peace. The German Underground Hospital is essential visiting for all with an interest in Jersey, the Second World War and the continuing struggle to achieve peace.

Parish of St. Lawrence

A view of St. Aubin's Bay from Mont Felard

The historic parish church of St. Lawrence

The 17th-century Le Rât Cottage

Touring by bike in the beautiful Waterworks Valley

A country path through the woods

St. Matthew's Glass Church: the glasswork was created by Frenchman René Lalique

Hamptonne

Country Life Museum

Jersey's verdant countryside

Potatoes cultivated under plastic, to protect them from the elements

AGRICULTURE

A bountiful island

The Jersey Royal: choice of the connoisseur

Fresh Jersey produce

A herd of superb Jersey cattle

Top-quality Jersey tomatoes for export

Most of Jersey's crops are destined for export. Yet the islanders still proudly recall their age-old ability to provide for themselves at the dinner table – a tradition born of necessity during hard times. These days, many of the island's 600 or so farms are growing tasty vegetables – especially potatoes and tomatoes – or raising the world-famous Jersey cow for its creamy milk.

When combined, agriculture and fishing today only account for around one percent of the island's revenue. But there have been agricultural booms. The cider industry flourished after King Charles II decreed that Jersey cider would be exempt from excise and one in four arable fields were planted with apple orchards. So popular was the island's cider by the late 19th century that Jersey was exporting some 150,000 gallons (680,000 litres) annually. Then, as new potatoes became a more popular crop, cider and cider vinegar production dropped as quickly as a falling apple. Local delicacies such as black butter – made with cider, apples and spices – are one of the few reminders of those prosperous years.

The premium export crop nowadays is the Jersey Royal new potato, making up nearly half of the island's agricultural income. Renowned for its waxy skin and unique nutty flavour, this kidney-shaped potato was 'discovered' by a local farmer in 1880. Within decades, this variety became a mainstay of the island's agricultural production and more than 40,000 tonnes are now exported annually. The island makes the most of its early spring, some three weeks in advance of the UK's, by shipping Jersey Royals from late February until mid-July. The Jersey Royal is recognised by Europe as a unique quality product and has been awarded the Protected Designation of Origin label – partly to protect its name from being misused and imitated by producers outside the island.

It is not just the warm surrounding seas and early spring that help Jersey's farmers. They till the south-facing plateau of fertile land to produce a variety of crops – among them tomatoes, sold from mid-March to mid-November, cauliflowers, courgettes, parsley, peppers and calabrese. At any one time, there are always at least three Jersey vegetable crops in season. New crops, such as runner beans, are being continually added to the list.

The Jersey cow, a breed found worldwide, is popular with visitors for its golden colour and come-hither eyes. Seen grazing in lush green fields island-wide, it is in fact the only cattle breed allowed here and once exported is not allowed to re-enter. Farmers admire this compact animal for

A young exhibitor

Agricultural show in Trinity

being the world's most-efficient and profitable dairy cow. Its rich and creamy milk, acclaimed for its high butterfat content, is also turned into a variety of other tasty dairy products.

The local seas, of course, teem with a variety of fish that grace some of the best restaurants in Jersey and beyond. Some 50 fishing boats still harvest bass, sole, bream, turbot, lobster and crab. Shellfish are also fished or cultivated locally – especially oysters, though unfortunately in much smaller quantities than in the past.

Horticulture too plays an important role in Jersey's agricultural economy. Flowers grown in gardens and greenhouses – among them daffodils, the main Jersey flower crop, as well as anemones, carnations, pinks, freesias, gladioli, irises, chrysanthemums and lilies – are shipped worldwide, often on the day they are cut. To celebrate their beauty, islanders organise colourful festivals such as the annual Battle of Flowers. Events like these highlight the continuing importance accorded by the people of Jersey to their fertile lands and bountiful seas.

The picturesque harbour of St. Aubin

Parish of
ST. BRELADE

Haven for
tourists and
wildlife

Village houses in St. Aubin

Located in the island's south-western corner, St. Brelade parish is renowned for its natural beauty – especially the fine beaches and imposing cliffs. Further noteworthy attractions include a lighthouse, standing sentinel for 130 years and reached by a path beloved of walkers and cyclists, massive fortifications from the last world war and one of only a handful of lavender farms still operating in the British Isles.

Looking out to the Atlantic, Corbière and its treacherous rocks were the undoing of many a ship until the construction of a lighthouse in the 19th century. The lighthouse was the first to be built of concrete in the British Isles and straddles a granite base only accessible at low tide. Many visitors arrive here from St. Aubin via the Railway Walk, a tree-lined path that once carried trains.

The picturesque tourist resort of St. Aubin, which looks eastwards across the bay of the same name, is famous for its fine hotels and restaurants, a spectacular beach and water sports. In the 18th century the town was more important than St. Helier, thanks to its safe and sheltered harbour – now filled with pleasure boats. Distinguished old merchants' houses bear witness to the town's original prosperity. A nearby islet accommodates a fort built in 1540 and further fortified by the German invaders.

Due south of St. Aubin lies Noirmont, a rocky headland now owned by the government and acting as an open-air memorial to islanders who perished in the last war. The promontory's strategic importance is confirmed by the presence of German-built bunkers and heavy artillery pieces – now preserved for posterity. Portelet Bay, the site of one of Jersey's smallest beaches, attracts those willing to brave the steep cliff paths. A Napoleonic-era defensive tower sits on an islet in the bay.

Across the headland, to the west, lies St. Brelade's Bay. It is home to one of the island's most popular beaches and also to some of the best hotels. The mainly Norman parish church, situated in the far west of the bay, has been extended down the centuries. Like several other churches on Jersey, it has a sanctuary path – the last thing seen by criminals who chose to leave the island rather than face harsh punishments. Next to the church is the Fisherman's Chapel, among the island's oldest Christian sanctuaries, containing recently restored medieval frescoes. Old and new sights and attractions can be found nearby. These range from menhirs (standing stones) dating back thousands of years to the exclusive La Moye Golf Club. Jersey Lavender Farm, which distils and bottles its own perfume, boasts gardens with over 70 species of the aromatic plant. Nature-lovers visit this parish for its superb flora and birds. Several rare species of both can be found in the grassy sand dunes close to La Rocco Tower, a Jersey round tower built in 1796 and now restored to its former glory. Evidence, as if it were needed, that this parish cherishes its history as much as its natural features.

Beauport

The 16th-century St. Aubin's Fort in St. Aubin's Bay

Belcroute Bay looking towards Noirmont

Janvrin's Tomb, in Portelet Bay

La Cotte Point

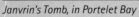

Parish of
ST. BRELADE

A young sand sculptress

Ouaisné Bay and St. Brelade's Bay

German World War Two coastal defences at Noirmont Point

THIS HEADLAND WAS ACQUIRED BY THE STATES OF JERSEY ON BEHALF OF THE PUBLIC IN COMMEMORATION OF THOSE MEN AND WOMEN OF JERSEY WHO PERISHED IN THE SECOND WORLD WAR 1939 — 1945

The Fisherman's Chapel in St. Brelade's Bay

The Shell Garden

Sand Racing in St. Ouen's Bay

Corbière lighthouse

Winston Churchill Memorial Park

Les Quennevais Lavender Farm

La Sergenté Neolithic passage grave

La Rocco Tower in St. Ouen's Bay

Summertime in St. Brelade's Bay

Parish of
ST. BRELADE

Gardens at St. Brelade's Bay

Under the Jersey sun

Cooling off

Heathland overlooking the dramatic coastline

Environment

Puffin in flight

Jersey is one of the last bastions of the Red Squirrel

Lapwing

The Jersey Orchid

A family of Shags

Dartford Warbler

The dunes close to Les Mielles

Gorse

Safeguarding nature's heritage

What draws so many people to Jersey is its magnificent environment. For such a small island, nature's beauty is displayed in an amazing variety of ways. The verdant countryside, wooded valleys, soaring cliffs, endless sandy beaches and rocky seascapes – all these and more are found in abundance here.

Wherever you are in the island, the sea is never far away. Its waters naturally dominate people's impressions of Jersey and are responsible for its very shape, separating it from the European continent some 8,000 years ago. Today, the sea still strongly influences the environment. Daily tides sweep around the 45 miles (72 km) of coastline, changing the island's aspect. The Bailiwick of Jersey actually doubles in size each day when the tide goes out, exposing vast areas of sand and rock that

are home to many plant and animal species. Over longer periods, especially given the large tidal flows of up to 40 feet (12 m), the coastal landscape of cliffs, caves and bays changes significantly.

The coastal zone is increasingly valued by Jersey. In the year 2000, over 12 square miles (32 sq. km) of unique coastal habitat on the island's southeast corner were designated as a United Nations 'Ramsar' wetland of international importance. The European Union also recognises the area as a priority marine ecosystem. The island's fragile dune systems – such as Les Blanches Banques, a Site of Special Interest accommodating some 400 different species of plant as well as green lizards and grass snakes and numerous bird species – are also carefully monitored, in order to minimise the impact of human activities and to control the

erosion of invasive plant species and noxious weeds. It is the job of local organisations, especially Jersey's Environmental Services Unit, to manage such zones and to protect the environment in general.

An ultraviolet sewage treatment plant helps ensure a pristine marine environment, which is so important for the booming sports and leisure sectors. Holidaymakers, surfers, windsurfers, anglers and divers, among others, rely on the surrounding seas being both clean and healthy. The island also has some of the cleanest beaches in Europe, according to annual international surveys.

Jersey has won international recognition for preserving the environment, including coveted Green Globe status for developing coastal footpaths and cycle tracks. The island is a walker's paradise, with everything from strolls in country lanes to the annual 48-mile (77 km) challenge of circumnavigating the coastline on foot. The popular Green Lane network, totalling some 45 miles (72 km) and copied elsewhere in the world, gives priority to walkers and cyclists over motorists.

Nature conservation is increasingly important here, with some 1,112 acres (450 hectares) of ecologically important habitats – including wetlands, woodland, maritime heath, sand dunes and grassland – managed by a team from the Environmental Services Unit. Three island locations are designated as ecological Sites of Special Interest, with another dozen likely to be added to the list in future. The ESU, as well as groups such as the Société Jersiaise and the National Trust for Jersey, regularly organise guided walks of such areas in addition to educational presentations and themed environment weekends designed to stimulate public interest.

Achieving a balance between development of the island and preservation of its environment will never be easy. Yet there is little doubt where the islanders' loyalty lies, for their government is a signatory to no fewer than 30 international conventions to safeguard the natural environment.

Far from the madding crowd

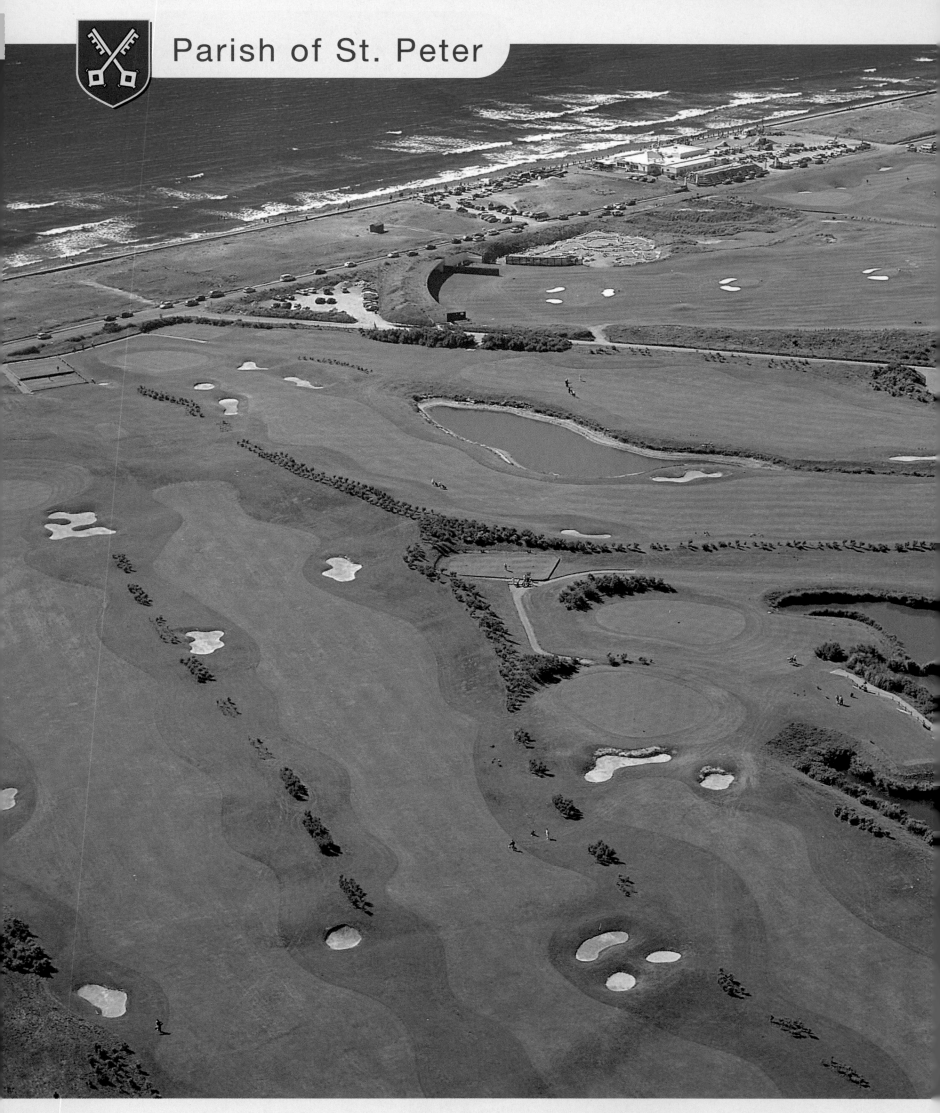

The International
Gateway

For many visitors, Jersey Airport is their first view of the island. Located in the heart of the parish of St. Peter, the airport has provided a vital transport link since 1937 and today sees some two million passengers pass through its gates every year. Yet the parish is also known for its beaches, its natural environment and quality tourist attractions.

Green Lanes, an early-1990s initiative by this parish, has now been copied by most others to create an island-wide network for recreational use. To discourage cars from using designated Green Lanes, authorities have set a top speed limit of 15 miles per hour (24 km/h), as opposed to the island maximum of 40 mph (64 km/h), and priority is given to pedestrians, cyclists and horse-riders.

The green theme continues in the conservation area of Les Mielles and St. Ouen's Pond (only half is in St. Peter's). Besides being rich in wildlife – especially seabirds, the area is home to some of the island's rarest plant species, such as the Jersey Pink. Nearby Les Mielles Golf and Country Club offers a challenging 18-hole parkland course.

Another popular area with walkers and nature enthusiasts is St. Peter's Valley. A stream flows through the wooded valley from its boundary with St. Mary's through to Beaumont on the south coast. The stream once powered several mills, but only Le Moulin de Quétivel now remains as a working mill, owned and maintained by the National Trust for Jersey. Le Val de la Mare, a valley in the west, today provides a reservoir (partly in St. Ouen's) and boasts a scenic perimeter walk.

As elsewhere in Jersey, the parish church, topped by the tallest spire of all the parochial churches, has been a focal point for housing development. Nearby is Le Manoir de la Hague, now home to a preparatory school and boasting a nature trail in its grounds.

A number of major attractions reside in this parish. They include the family-owned Sunset Nurseries, a business that sells and delivers fresh flowers grown on the premises in large greenhouses. It is popular with visitors, especially for its tropical bird garden. The Living Legend offers a programme recreating scenes from the island's history with stunning special effects, while providing a range of other facilities such as large landscaped gardens. Lastly, the Star and Tipsy Toad is a unique public house and brewery, based in St. Peter's Village, producing traditional cask-conditioned real ales. All these places are good additional reasons to dwell a little longer in this gateway parish.

Les Mielles, a golfers' paradise

One of the larger parishes, it shares borders with St. Ouen and St. Mary to the north and with St. Lawrence to the east. It uniquely shares a border with St. Brelade to the south and is the only parish to have two separate seaboards – in the west, at St. Ouen's Bay, and in the south at St. Aubin's Bay. From St. Peter's western border, the land rises over sand dunes to the higher plateau on which the airport has been built. The parish is still largely given over to agriculture, with farmers producing a range of crops and managing dairy herds.

The Living Legend attraction

La caumine à Marie Best: 18th century guardhouse and powder magazine

St. Peter's Parish Church, with the tallest spire (120 ft, 37 m) in Jersey

MGs past and present on display at the Jersey Rugby Club

Parish of St. Peter

St. Peter's Valley

The Star and Tipsy Toad pub and brewery

Jet-skiing in St. Aubin's Bay

Windmill Inn

Sunset Nurseries

A 450 year-old cannon at Beaumont crossroads

Val de la Mare reservoir (half in St. Ouen)

Le Moulin de Quétivel

An airport for the international traveller

Departure terminal – heart of the airport

Flying High

Aviation and the horse and carriage era came face to face in Jersey on 31 August 1912 when Frenchman Jean Benoist landed his biplane on the beach at St. Aubin's Bay. He led the first leg of an air race from St. Malo on the nearby French coast but sadly finished third when an inquisitive crowd delayed his departure. Early commercial flying at Jersey centred on West Park beach and St. Helier Harbour,

where amphibious craft were often seen. By the late 1920s, when regular services were operating from the beach outside the capital, St. Helier, the machines were still regarded with a mixture of suspicion and fascination by the general population. However, the business community marvelled at the rapidity of passenger and mail transportation and its beneficial impact on trade. It was the traders,

through the Chamber of Commerce, who urged the building of a permanent airport. The island government – known as the States of Jersey – is normally a conservative body. But it looked to the future and responded to these demands, despite misgivings about the cost and public opposition. The airport was built on its current site in the west of the island, opening for business in March 1937. Over the years, the airport's early visionaries have been vindicated. Island communities everywhere are dependent on excellent transport communications. This is particularly so in Jersey, which has an economy based on business. The airport has played a very important part in the Island's economic development – especially the tourism and finance industries, which both require efficient and comprehensive air-transport systems.

From the outset, islanders enjoyed easier contact with the UK mainland through an increase in daily mail deliveries. Those in agriculture, then the principal industry, had speedy access to markets for their early crops. By November 1938, some 35,000 passengers had been carried, making Jersey the UK's second busiest airport in terms of passenger traffic to London (Croydon). Moreover, the relative isolation of residents was broken, a change not appreciated by all. The success was short-lived, as the airport came under the control of the Luftwaffe during the Second World War.

By the 1940s, Jersey had, in a small but significant way, been on the UK tourist map for over a hundred years. It was well served by steamers from ports in southern England. Yet the airport, still

Jersey Airport

Last-minute gifts

Good-value shopping

viewed by some as a burden on the public purse, came into its own after the Occupation years. As normal service resumed, a veritable explosion of air travel occurred with former military airfields, aircraft and crews on the mainland providing the raw material for more affordable air travel.

Jersey Airport became the catalyst for the Island's fledgling modern tourism industry, bringing much-needed income to a community striving to overcome the strife of Occupation and to compete in the modern world. Air passenger numbers leapt from 65,000 in 1946 to 113,000 in 1947, leading to predictions, which were confirmed nine years later, that air travel would overtake the sea as the most common form of passenger transport. Tourism, principally from the UK, was the driving force of the Jersey economy by the late 1960s. Consistently, surveys carried out by the Jersey Tourism Department reveal that 75% of leisure visitors to the island cite the availability of flights from their local airport as a major factor in their decision to visit.

The demise of agriculture as a major industry and the dependency on tourism, with its intensive servicing and infrastructure requirements, pushed the airport's role further to the core of island life when the States, again with considerable foresight, sought to create a third pillar of the economy. The government established the now flourishing finance industry, for which excellent transport links are essential.

Residents of Jersey today enjoy a high standard of living, with an economy greatly dependent on ease of communication including aviation. So it is tempting to believe that they have always appreciated their airport. However, developments there have not always been greeted with the same enthusiasm as the economic rewards. Most resistance to improvement schemes has hinged on the need to use more land. This is habitually challenged in any farming community, but in Jersey, with restricted land resources, resistance tends to be particularly strong.

Many political battles have been fought to achieve improvements to the size and construction of the runway and taxiways, the building of hangars and extensions to the terminal buildings, plus extensive investment in safety and navigational aids. The introduction of jet aircraft in the 1960s resulted in a protracted noise-control campaign. It has been

the Island's good fortune that successive administrations have, in the face of sometimes fierce opposition, continued to provide a safe and secure environment to meet its air-transport needs and ensure that all operations undertaken are within the social, economic and environmental policies as determined by the States of Jersey.

Jersey Airport has for decades operated the Air Traffic Control service in the Channel Islands Control Zone, on behalf of the UK and French governments. The zone is a block of air space up to 20,000 feet and extends from off the Brittany coast of France to a line to the north, midway across the English Channel. The management of this busy sector encompasses not only approach control for the airports of Jersey, Guernsey and Alderney, but also the safe passage of aircraft flying through it to UK and Europe.

Commercial flights operate between Jersey and around 80 UK and Continental towns and cities every year. Annual passenger throughput grew to 2 million by 1990 and some 60% of air travellers pass through the airport on the peak summer weekends. March 1997 saw the completion of a £23-million development – including a new departures terminal, new baggage reclaim hall and substantial improvement to roadways and car parks – to coincide with the sixtieth birthday of the original airport. Due to "global shrinking", fewer tourists now choose Jersey as their main holiday destination. Inevitably, passenger numbers have

fallen, to around 1.7 million. Some year-round routes have been lost and the public clamour for ever-lower airfares does not sit easily with the desire to sustain the mature all-year route network. This is the challenge for today's Island leaders. Thanks to their predecessors' foresight, they can rest assured that the airport is able to meet Jersey's aviation needs well into the new millennium.

End of another busy day at Jersey Airport

Hub for both commercial and executive aviation

Serving the business community

Established in Jersey for more than three decades, Aviation Beauport Limited is the island's premier air taxi and charter operator. A fleet of modern aircraft, such as the latest Citation business jet, is always on hand to serve busy clients travelling throughout Europe and beyond. Companies in the Group also handle everything from aircraft sales and management to handling and maintenance.

Aviation Beauport is based at Jersey International Airport, a few miles west of the island's capital, St. Helier. The majority of its clients are business people, working in Jersey or travelling there from the Continent for meetings.

Flexibility is one of the Jersey company's key assets. It is unhampered by the restrictions of traditional scheduled services – whose destinations or times may not suit passengers or which may be cancelled due to inclement weather. Even at short notice, Aviation Beauport is able to provide Europe-wide flights, by day or night. It can also conveniently set down at or take off from airports not served by regular airlines, facilitating life for business people working to tight timetables. A chartered flight, moreover, offers passengers the sort of security and privacy to work that they cannot find on scheduled services. The company can comfortably fly up to 20 passengers, calling on any of several modern aircraft. Its own fleet includes a Citation 2 Corporate Jet and two Cessna 310s. Under its corporate management programme, the company also operates a number of other corporate jets – among them an HS 125, a Citation 1 and a Citation Excel – on behalf of their owners. Corporate management provides huge benefits for aircraft-owners, removing the hassles associated with owning and running an aircraft. The Excel, the fleet's most recent addition, is the first business jet in its class to offer passengers a cabin in which they can stand up. The well-appointed aircraft is ideal for both business and leisure travel, accommodating up to eight passengers in style and comfort. With a full payload, the Excel has a range of some 1,800 miles – a distance that would take in northern Africa for example or Moscow to the east – and cruises at nearly 500 miles per hour.

Besides air charter and corporate management, the company's highly successful and core businesses, Aviation Beauport offers dedicated handling facilities. Services available – for everything from a single-engined Piper to a Boeing business jet – include flight planning and despatch, weather briefing, slot handling and third-party handling, fuel uplifts, aircraft valeting and hangarage. Experienced and courteous staff are also adept at booking hotels and limousines, organising catering – for instance at the company's own luxurious meeting facilities, assisting with ground power units and engineering, and providing air ambulance flights. Last but not least, group member Jersey Aircraft Maintenance Limited has international approvals to service a wide range of aircraft at its well-equipped and state-of-the-art facility.

Whatever their reasons for travelling to or from Jersey, passengers availing themselves of the services of Aviation Beauport can rest assured that their journeys will be relaxing and stress-free – and above all time and cost-effective.

Keeping the island warm

Powering the island's growth

Fuel Supplies (C.I.) Limited, a wholly owned subsidiary of Shell, is Jersey's leading supplier of energy, oil and heating services. Founded in 1955, the dynamic company has invested extensively in developing storage and distribution systems to meet energy demands and today serves customers in homes, businesses and industry. It is also the exclusive fuel distributor to Jersey Airport, refuelling the aircraft that play such an important role in the local economy.

From its base at the port facilities in La Collette, St. Helier, Fuel Supplies daily sends out its familiar yellow tankers to customers across the island. Many of them are homeowners already convinced of the benefits – in terms of choice, convenience and economy – of oil-fired central heating. Though the company has been the main supplier of heating oil for over four decades, its drive for excellence continues to result in the development of innovative services. These include the design and installation of heating systems, boiler maintenance and insur-

Exclusive fuel distributors to Jersey International Airport

ance, a full plumbing service and oil storage tank replacement.

Professional advice on energy conservation and fuel consumption is readily available to all customers, underlining the company's commitment to responsible and environmentally conscious use of energy. For those seeking peace of mind, the company also offers planned payment and delivery facilities.

Garage forecourts across the length and breadth of the island remain an important market for the company. Their own clients, whether local motorists or visitors, have warmly welcomed the services offered to holders of the Shell Card – now widely accepted as an ideal way of purchasing motor as well as marine and aviation fuel, whilst enjoying significant card membership benefits.

Fuel Supplies continually develops and diversifies the Card's range of redemption opportunities.

In addition to serving businesses across the island, notably the increasing numbers of international finance and professional institutions, the company has worked hard to keep pace with growth in the tourism and hospitality sector. Numerous hotels, restaurants and shops rely on it for a comfortable and healthy working environment. Farmers and growers too, not to mention Jersey's fishing fleet, depend on the quality of Shell fuels and lubricants for their livelihoods and safety. Direct access to the comprehensive resources of Shell enables the company to support a wide range of machinery by offering highly specialised oils, fluids and greases to meet manufacturers' specifications.

At Jersey Airport, Fuel Supplies annually pumps up to 15 million litres of aviation fuel to more than 100 customers. Facilities include an on-site fuel farm with storage for some 500,000 litres of aviation fuel, plus a fleet of nine tankers for interplaning operations. At peak periods, the firm is called on to refuel as many as 200 aircraft daily, ranging from small Cessnas to large passenger jets. General aviation aircraft based at the Jersey Aero Club are also serviced by the same dedicated team.

Proud of its long tradition of service and involvement within the Jersey community, Fuel Supplies is as determined as ever to keep the wheels of industry and commerce turning and to meet the increasingly sophisticated demands of all its clients.

Reliably serving the island's farmers and growers

129

Powering the island

First introduced into Jersey in the 1830s for street lighting, gas has played a major and expanding role in the island's development. Today, Jersey Gas Company continues to provide residents and businesses with this safe, clean and convenient fuel, used for a wide range of heating, cooking, transport and leisure requirements.

Until the 1960s, all local gas was generated from coal at a production plant in St. Helier. Nowadays, mains gas is manufactured from liquefied petroleum gas (LPG), butane and propane. Besides improving both the quality and safety of the fuel, this change, completed in 1977, paved the way for the introduction of a modern range of gas appliances.

Gas is imported into Jersey, in liquid form, by specially constructed ships. It is stored in large vessels before being used to produce a manufactured gas, which is then piped across the island to domestic and commercial customers. Liquid propane and butane are also filled into cylinders which are then distributed all over the island by road tankers, for delivery to customers able to store the fuel in mini bulk-tanks.

Jersey Gas was the first company in the British Isles to use the new gas mains insertion technique called Sub Coil. Allowing long lengths of new plastic pipe to be inserted through old pipe, this is a quick method of replacing pipe and reducing maintenance costs and inconvenience to the public.

Jersey Gas – responsible for providing all the island's gas – is part of the International Energy Group, which has operations in the Channel Islands, the UK, Portugal and the Isle of Man. The company employs over 90 people and is based at an administration office and showroom in St. Helier. It has a modern gas-making plant at the nearby site of La Collette, and a bottle-filling plant in the northern parish of St. John. Distribution is via a gas mains network, totalling some 290 km in length, or by cylinders or bulk through the sister company Kosangas. Based in St. John, Kosangas offers an LPG filling and distribution service for customers located beyond the mains network; it also supplies and delivers CO2 and various other industrial gases.

Because the gas used in the island's mains distribution network is a manufactured LPG/Air mixture, all gas appliances imported into Jersey for use on this network require conversion. This is carried out by Jersey Gas's qualified staff, who are able to modify and test equipment.

The company retails a wide range of modern appliances, for both mains gas and LPG, meeting the needs of domestic and commercial customers. The range covers central heating boilers and systems, space and water heating, as well as equipment for cooking and leisure activities – such as gas-fired barbecues and patio heaters. On the commercial side, appliances are available to cater to all the cooking and heating requirements of hotels and restaurants.

More sophisticated gas-fired equipment includes highly efficient Combined Heat and Power (CHP) systems. Sometimes likened to a miniature power station, a CHP plant is ideal for supplying electrical power and heat to a building or swimming pool. Jersey is already home to five CHP units, at two hotels, a leisure complex, a farm and a school. Also available are boilers that provide carbon dioxide enrichment to greenhouse crops and chillers used in air conditioning.

The sister company Kosangas also helps to put the bubbles in various soft drinks and beer, by extracting nitrogen from the air and storing this gas in cylinders for distribution. Various other gases are made available to industries involved in welding, food packaging and brewing.

Jersey Gas takes pride in its fleet of vehicles, most of which now operate on LPG Autogas, otherwise known as propane. More than 33 Jersey Gas vehicles run on this energy-saving road fuel, with others shortly coming on stream. Autogas offers a number of benefits over conventional fuels such as petrol and diesel, among them lower vehicle running costs. It also produces fewer harmful emissions and is therefore kinder to the environment and people's health – something considered important in the lovely island of Jersey. Some five million vehicles worldwide now run on this fuel. That figure is likely to increase significantly, thanks to growing environmental awareness and a plethora of new fiscal incentives offered by wise governments. Jersey, for instance, currently exempts Autogas from duty.

The company is geared to help fleet operators that may be interested in converting their own vehicles to run on Autogas – for example by siting storage tanks and dispensers in convenient locations. Local garages with trained staff can also convert most types of existing vehicle to use this environmentally friendly new fuel, and service them too. The island currently has two outlets for Autogas: a refuelling station in St. Helier run by Jersey Gas and another in Trinity, managed by Freelance Motor Group.

Fully committed to the satisfaction of its customers, Jersey Gas provides a low-rate gas tariff to anyone who uses gas for heating. The tariff can also be used for fires and associated gas appliances, such as cookers and water heaters.

Jersey Gas is fully integrated into the island way of life, providing an emergency service equal to those provided in far larger environments. Commitment to ever-improving standards is seen as the best way to provide a secure long-term service.

So some 170 years after its arrival in Jersey, gas and its various derivatives play a more important role than ever in powering the island, empowering its population and helping to preserve the island's beauty.

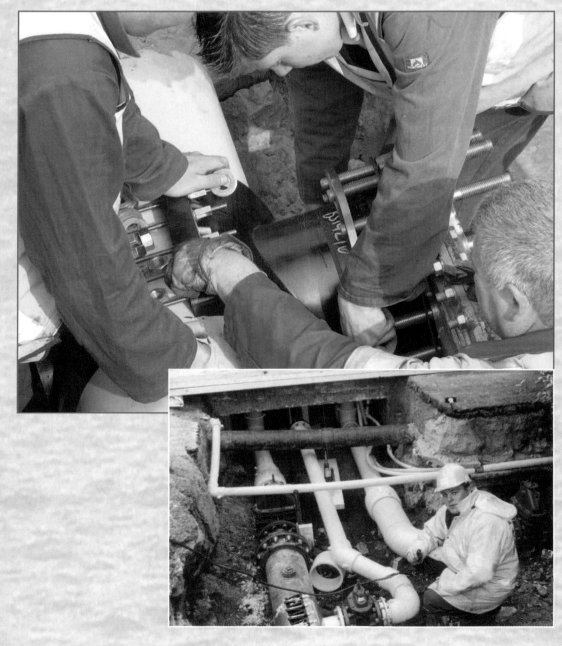

A tradition of excellence

Jersey Mutual Insurance Society prides itself on serving the people of Jersey, from its modern premises in central St. Helier. Established more than 130 years ago and today the only home-grown insurance company, it has gathered substantial experience of the island, its conditions and inhabitants – experience which is harnessed by offering members a better service at unrivalled rates. Considerable financial strength in the form of large reserves and established reinsurance arrangements, coupled with an exclusive range of household insurance products, make the Society a highly attractive proposition.

As the main provider of household insurance to residents of Jersey, the Society enjoys an enviable reputation. Tradition underpins its service offerings: all new clients receive a personal visit by a Director of the company, in order to determine suitable levels of insurance. Should a claim ever be made, that same person will visit again and promptly resolve the matter. Each parish on the island is served by two dedicated Directors.

Because of its mutual status, Jersey Mutual holds all policies directly rather than working through a broker. This means there are no dividends paid to shareholders and no commissions paid to agents. Policyholders – who are all members – therefore pay lower premiums, without losing any cover.

The Society uniquely specialises in household insurance, which covers homes and the contents therein on a new for old basis against loss or damage from many insured events, such as fire, floods, theft, impact and subsidence. An optional extra for those who insure their home contents is cover for Personal Possessions. This means that household insurance provides All Risks cover on items such as jewellery, personal effects, clothing and baggage

Local household insurance specialist

for items worth up to a pre-arranged limit. Specified items, worth more than the pre-arranged limit, can also be covered. Personal Possessions cover protects members who are away from home for accidental loss or damage anywhere in the Channel Islands, British Isles and Europe, plus up to 60 days anywhere else in the world.

Whether at home or travelling, members of Jersey Mutual can rest assured all their insurance needs are comprehensively met today and in the future.

Head Office of Jersey Mutual

Serving the people of Jersey since 1869

The spectacular beauty of St. Ouen's Bay

Windsurfing in St. Ouen's Bay

Parish of St. Ouen

Something for everyone

The largest of the 12 parishes, St. Ouen occupies the island's north-west corner. It is known for its fine beaches and as a haven for wild flowers and birds. Agriculture remains the principal industry, with south-facing slopes used for the cultivation of Jersey Royal new potatoes and higher land for mixed farming.

The northern side has two small sandy bays. La Grève de Lecq (partly in St. Mary's) attracts many bathers, while its harbour is favoured by small fishing boats. To the west lies Plémont Bay: its beach, arguably Jersey's finest, is only accessible at low tide. A granite pillar, the much-photographed Needle Rock, adorns the entrance to one of the caves here.

The north-western headland of Grosnez has a ruined castle, dating from the 14th-century. Local people sheltered there during French invasions.

Turning south, the coast is dotted with World War Two German fortifications, some now restored. Just inland is Les Landes, made up of gorse and heather. The rugged moorland surrounds Jersey Race Course, which hosts horse race meetings between April and September.

Peaceful Plémont Bay

The coastline falls steeply to L'Etacq, home to a small jetty used by fishing boats. St. Ouen's Bay, parts of which traverse the parishes of St. Peter and St. Brelade, dominates Jersey's western seaboard. The vast beach here draws many surfers and sailboarders keen to ride the Atlantic rollers, sometimes for major championships, as well as sand yachting devotees.

Running along the bay, Five Mile Road – which is just over three miles in length – is fronted by several 19th-century fortifications. One of these, Kempt Tower, has an information centre for visitors interested in the bay and surrounding area. The tower makes a good starting point for walkers discovering the diverse plant, animal and bird life on the inland coastal plain – especially at Les Mielles (meaning sand dunes), a popular nature conservation area. Nearby St. Ouen's Pond (partly in St. Peter's) is the island's largest stretch of natural freshwater. It is owned by the National Trust for Jersey and provides a valuable habitat for numerous birds.

Those with an interest in archaeology should see the Monts Grantez dolmen, a typical Neolithic passage grave. Le Pinacle, the natural pinnacle rock in the Les Landes area, rises some 200 feet (60 m) above sea level. Excavations revealed the traces of various settlements here, stretching back some 3,000 years.

Home to the influential de Carteret family since 1135, St. Ouen's Manor stands in the heart of the parish. Members of the family – which once owned the 11th-century parish church – have often worked as administrators for St. Ouen and the island. Two other surviving manors, Vinchelez de Haut and Vinchelez de Bas, flank the main road to Grosnez Castle.

Housed in a restored bunker on Five Mile Road, the Channel Islands Military Museum displays British and German World War Two equipment. The Battle of Flowers Museum, founded by experienced flower-float builder Florence Bechelet, displays her work from this unique Jersey festival. Visitors seeking special gifts should check out Bouchet Agateware Pottery, offering a multitude of designs created by a local potter.

The island's local language, Jersey Norman-French, is still spoken by many in this parish. Its famous son, the late Dr Frank Le Maistre, compiled the popular Jèrriais-English dictionary.

Family fun

Fertile farmland

St. Ouen's Pond Nature Reserve straddles the border with St.Peter's parish

Route de l'Etacq

Respect for other toad users!

Parish of
St. Ouen

The 12th-century Moulin de Lecq Inn

18th-century Square Fort

Five Mile Road

Channel Islands Military Museum, situated in old WW2 bunker

Kempt Tower and Les Mielles Visitor's centre

St. Ouen's Manor

L'Etacq

The coast at Les Squez

The Bouchet Agateware Pottery

The WW2 German Battery at Les Landes

Le Pulec

St. Ouen's Parish Hall

Looking for a winner

Racing at Les Landes

Grève de Lecq beach: stream running through the sea wall marks the parish boundary with St.Mary's

Ruins of the 14th-century Grosnez Castle

Grosnez Point

The Pinacle

Parish of
St. Ouen

Natural beauty and charm

The majestic beauty of the coast at Le Câtel de Lecq

Parish of St. Mary

St. Mary's is home to fewer than 1,600 residents and is the island's second smallest parish. Yet this very rural area attracts many visitors, who come to admire its spectacular coastline of steep cliffs lashed by Atlantic breakers. Situated in the northwest of the island, it shares borders with the parishes of St. Ouen, St. Peter, St. Lawrence and St. John.

Natural beauty as well as superb views of the sea draw thousands of people to the coast here. Their footsteps trace a path running from Mourier Val-

The coast at Devil's Hole

cave's roof collapsed and is constantly pounded by the open sea. Half a mile westwards lies Ile Agois, a small offshore stack separated from the coast by a deep gorge. Traces of former settlements have been found on the islet, including the remains of circular prehistoric huts.

On the headland above Grève de Lecq, there are several rifle ranges used for fullbore, smallbore, pistol and clay pigeon events. Jersey has produced many international champions at shooting. Practice of the sport probably stems from the days of the Jersey Militia, when all men were required to undertake shooting drill on a Sunday. Just inland lie the Grève de Lecq barracks, built during the early 19th century to help fend off any possible French attacks. Now owned by the National Trust for Jersey, which has its headquarters in this parish, the barracks contain an information display on the bay's military and social past, the north coast footpaths and wildlife.

Climbing enthusiasts have the choice of many fine

A walk on the beach

locations, both in Mourier Valley and along the granite sea cliffs. Other popular activities, in addition to walking, are swimming and surfing at Grève de Lecq.

St. Mary village includes a parish church, rectory, parish hall, junior school and public house – all within half a mile of each other, as well as a new youth and community centre.

Set on high ground, the land here is mainly given over to arable farming, although there are some glasshouse growers. One of these has diversified by including rare and exotic butterflies in his glasshouses. Jersey Butterfly Centre, which stands next to a traditional 17th-century farmhouse, is now a popular tourist attraction.

The land at La Mare Vineyards has long been planted with vines and is an established producer of local wine, brandy and preserves. Visitors can see the process of winemaking and distilling and enjoy the vineyards, orchards and gardens. Like the parish itself, this is a place to sample at first hand.

ley in the east, the dividing line between this parish and St. John's, to the sandy bay of Grève de Lecq in the west. The popular beach here is split between the parishes of St. Mary and St. Ouen, their boundary marked by the stream that comes down the valley and passes through a hole in the sea wall.

The parish's best-known sight is Devil's Hole, shaped like a deep funnel some 100 feet (30 m) across and etched into a cliff south-east of Mourier Valley. It came into being when a former

Grève de Lecq: parish boundary with St. Ouen's is marked by the stream that runs through the sea wall

The Butterfly Centre

Parish of St. Mary

Strolling with friends

La Mare Vineyard

St. Mary's Parish Church

Rural St. Mary's

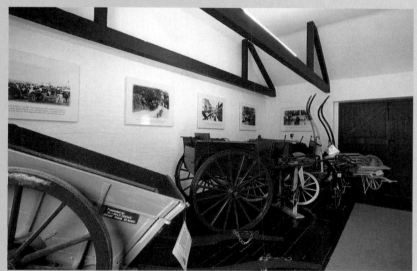

Exhibition of horse-drawn vehicles on display at the barracks

The Devil keeps watch

Parish boundary marker

Grève de Lecq Barracks: completed in 1815 and now fully restored

Parish of
St. John
In harmony with nature

St John's Parish Church

The northernmost of Jersey's parishes, St. John – historically known as St. John in the Oaks – is one of the island's least densely populated. It has a rugged coastline, affording fine views of the other Channel Islands when the weather permits. Lying on high ground, the land here is best suited to cattle farming and arable agriculture. The parish crest features a silver Maltese Cross, emblem of the Knights of St. John of Jerusalem.

Island centre stone at Sion

The only beach of note is found at Bonne Nuit Bay. It supposedly takes its name ('good night' in English) from a comment uttered by Charles II, who was soon to be king of England, when he departed from here for exile in France. Standing sentinel in the middle of the bay is the Cheval Roc: islanders used to row around it on Midsummer's Day to stave off bad luck.

The picturesque bay provides shelter for local fishing boats, who put into the small harbour built in the mid-19th century. It also attracts sporting crowds every summer. They come to cheer on the brave souls who compete in the Channel Islands' premier rowing race – a distance of some 19 nautical miles from Sark to Jersey. The winners complete the course in around two hours. First held in 1967, this popular event features single rowers, pairs and teams of four.

Just west of here and set below steep cliffs lie the Wolf's Caves, today a tourist attraction but formerly used by smugglers to store their illegal goods. One legend says the caves get their name from scary tales spread around by the smugglers themselves in order to keep away the local population.

Potato cultivation

Transmitter masts make good use of the high point at Fremont, just inland. The headland at Sorel was the site for the most southerly beacon lit in Britain, celebrating Queen Elizabeth's golden jubilee in 2002.

Quarries once played a major role in the whole island's economy, but only a couple of commercial operations remain. The company at Ronez Point has extracted granite here for over a hundred years. It also recently provided each parish's millennium standing stone, which together form a sort of modern megalithic network.

Material for the island's millennium granite crosses also hails from a quarry in this parish. The local cross is sited alongside La Route du Nord, with the sea providing a magnificent backdrop. Constructed during the German occupation of Jersey, this road was one of the work schemes invented by the island authorities to prevent unemployed islanders from working for the occupiers.

The village of St. John has developed around its 11th-century parish church. Its cemetery contains the grave of the parish's best-known benefactor, Sir Billy Butlin, founder of Butlin's holiday camps. His tombstone includes an engraving of an amusement park. Nearby St. John's Manor boasts magnificent grounds, but is unfortunately not generally open to the public.

The parish has one other claim to fame. For it is home to the Centre Stone, close to the village of Sion, said to indicate the island's geographic centre.

Farming country

Bonne Nuit Bay looking eastwards towards Trinity

The legendary Cheval Roc in Bonne Nuit Bay

Bonne Nuit Bay

Charming Rozel Bay: the parish boundary with St. Martin runs across the beach

Parish of Trinity

A style of its own

A large but sparsely populated parish, Trinity lies in the north of the island and is best known for its splendid beaches and the Jersey Zoo, founded by naturalist Gerald Durrell.

Flanked by steep cliffs, the beach at Bouley Bay is a magnet to holidaymakers, not to mention scuba divers, rock climbers and fishing enthusiasts. Local fishing boats also make use of the harbour. The steep hill rising out of the bay is

used by the Jersey Motor Cycle and Light Car Club for hill climbs several times a year. Walkers prefer to take to the cliff-top paths that stretch to the east and west of this parish.

Les Platons, the island's highest point at some 454 feet (138 metres) above sea level, lies just behind the panoramic promontory at Belle Hougue Point. Several radio and television transmitter masts are sited nearby, making good use

species back into the wild. A number of other destinations are also noteworthy. The Howard Davis Farm, situated alongside the parish church, was a bequest to the island from one of its great philanthropists, T.B. Davis, in memory of his son who was killed during the First World War. The farm – which houses the island's Agriculture and Fisheries Department and offices for the World Jersey Cattle Bureau – does a wide range of research into plants and crops. The Royal Jersey Agricultural and Horticultural Society has recently been established nearby.

Situated on the parish's western fringe, the Pallot Steam Museum presents a fascinating collection of steam engines, agricultural implements and other machinery.

The museum's founder worked as a trainee engineer on the old Jersey Railway. On the other side of the parish, near Victoria Village, the Eric Young Orchid Foundation is also popular with visitors. A series of large greenhouses – each with its own climate and lighting – house more than 20,000 species of this exquisite flower. Established in 1958, this unique centre includes a purpose-built nursery and exhibition complex, and has won many international awards for the orchids it grows.

Many of the older buildings in this parish are traditional Jersey farmhouses. Trinity Manor, however, was extensively altered in the early 20th century and is an impressive residence more French than Jersey in character. The manor's Seigneurs traditionally pay homage to Her Majesty the Queen when she visits Jersey and the custom is for the Seigneur of Trinity to present a pair of mallard ducks to the sovereign. For a beautiful parish like this, putting its best foot forward comes as second nature.

of the north coast's altitude. Internationally famous for its pioneering animal conservation work, Jersey Zoo has attracted millions of visitors since it opened in 1963. The zoo, which is the headquarters of the Durrell Wildlife Conservation Trust, is based at Les Augrès Manor and Les Noyers, on the eastern side of the parish. The Trust's main work is with endangered species and visitors here will see for themselves the success in breeding species such as the Lowland Gorillas and Spectacled Bears, as well as many smaller mammals, birds and reptiles. Les Noyers, the educational centre, is used to train conservationists from around the world in the techniques and skills of breeding and releasing endangered

Trinity's unspoiled coastline

Bouley Bay

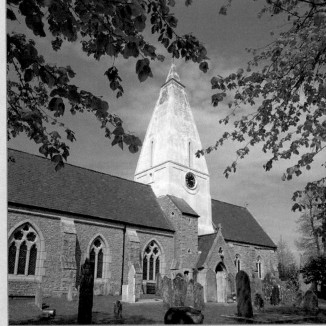
Trinity Parish Church

Les Platons, Jersey's highest point, at 454 feet (138 m) above sea level

Jardin d'Olivet, scene of a 16th-century battle with the French

Giffard Bay

Please Drive
With Care
Ducks And Geese
On Road

A faithful friend

The beach at Rozel Bay

Parish of **Trinity**

A taste of yesteryear, at the Pallot Steam Museum

Pallot Steam Museum

The Eric Young Orchid Foundation

149

Lifeline for endangered species

Jersey Zoo and Durrell Wildlife Conservation Trust

Gerald Durrell

Attracting over a quarter of a million visitors every year, Jersey Zoo is one of the island's most popular destinations. The Zoo is home to more than 100 endangered animal species, many of these among the rarest in the world, and has acquired an international reputation for its efforts to rescue creatures on the brink of extinction.

Located in Trinity parish, this unique zoo was the brainchild of author and naturalist Gerald Durrell (1925-1995). His decision to settle in Jersey, in 1959, came after a decade spent scouring the world for endangered animals. Durrell's dream, soon to come true, was to help such species to recover on the island and then to return them to the wild wherever possible.

The Zoo itself has gradually grown up around Les Augrès Manor, an elegant 18th-century building made of local granite. The manor is set in some 13 hectares of parkland and landscaped gardens, which contain rare and exotic flowers, shrubs and trees. The animals - including mammals, birds and reptiles – live within this area, in a variety of enclosures and open areas which mimic their natural habitats. Visitors can wander round the Zoo at their leisure, admiring apes such as the gorillas and orang-utangs in their purpose-built spacious surroundings, or the many different kinds of bird flying around their specially designed aviaries. A range of modern facilities, among them a visitor centre, restaurant and gift shop, also enhances people's experience of the Zoo.

Yet this is a zoo with a difference. While warmly welcoming all visitors, the establishment focuses on its animals and their welfare. The reason is simple: Jersey Zoo is also famous as the headquarters of the Durrell Wildlife Conservation Trust. Set up in 1963, this charity has carved out an enviable reputation for saving animals from oblivion. Its watchword, Saving species worldwide, speaks volumes about its goals. Over the last four decades, it has pioneered conservation programmes both in Jersey and overseas. Indeed, several endangered species owe their continued existence to this vigilant organisation. Its dodo logo remains a poignant and painful reminder of what happens when such animals are not protected.

Durrell Wildlife, as it calls itself, started out by res-

A majestic gorilla

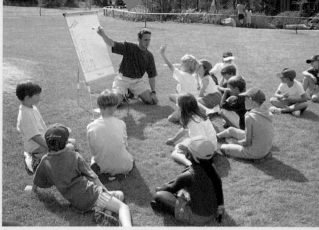

Sumatran Orang-utang

Overseas Conservation Programme

The gorilla enclosure

cuing endangered animals and bringing them back to Jersey. A wide range of species, from apes to iguanas, have come through the gates over the last four decades. Some are refugees from natural disasters, such as floods or volcanic eruptions. The others, unfortunately in the majority these days, are the victims of human encroachment on their home territory. In all cases, however, the aim is to save survivors and breed animals that can be returned to the wild.

Captive breeding is easier said than done, especially when you only have a few individuals in your collection. Thanks to trial and error, and a good dose of scientific expertise, the trust has succeeded in breeding species – such as the Poison-Dart Frog

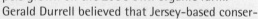

Golden-Headed Lion Tamarin

from the South American rainforests and the St. Lucia parrot – never previously raised in captivity. To ensure every species is given the best possible care, the Trust employs 'keeper scientists' – experts capable of doing much more than a traditional zoo-keeper. A team of full-time vets is also on hand, working from modern on-site facilities. As for housing and diets, each animal is given shelter and food closely matching that in their natural environment. Gibbons, for instance, live happily alongside orang-utangs, as happens in the wild. And picky parakeets are dished up tasty peppers grown on the Zoo's own organic farm.

Gerald Durrell believed that Jersey-based conser-

vation was only a first step. Which is why Durrell Wildlife increasingly works directly with endangered species in their own countries. One notable success is the Mauritius Kestrel. Once reduced to just four known individuals in the wild, the world's rarest kestrel is now thriving at home with 850 flying free. A 20-year campaign to increase numbers of the rare Pink Pigeon, also from Mauritius, is now paying dividends too. Many other species, including reptiles and mammals, have enjoyed similar breeding and recovery help from this trust. Aid also extends to advising local populations on ways of protecting natural environments, to help both animals and people.

Thanks to the Trust's on-site 'university', the International Training Centre, over 1,000 young people from all over the world have graduated with expertise in conservation and captive breeding. They enthusiastically spread the good word, not only about the marvellous work done at Jersey Zoo but also about saving endangered species on our increasingly fragile planet.

Echo Parakeet

Golden Poison-Dart Frog

Watching the world go by

The graceful flamingos

Parish of
St. MARTIN

Historic Reflections

Home to the medieval castle at Gorey, the north-eastern parish of St. Martin is renowned for its beaches and coastline. The numerous bays and coves draw droves of tourists all year round. However, most of the parish's income is generated by agriculture, with the south-facing slopes used for early new potatoes and the higher land for cattle and arable farming.

Mont Orgueil Castle is the most prominent feature in St. Martin's. This vast fortification – also known as Gorey Castle – owes its existence to the proximity of the once-threatening French. The first stones were laid in the 13th century, although additional building continued for many years. French invaders attacked the castle on several occasions, and even occupied it for seven years in the 15th century. The fort became redundant after

the introduction of cannon, but was saved from destruction by the island's governor Sir Walter Raleigh. It passed into the hands of Royalists then Parliamentarians during the English Civil War and formed a key part of the German occupiers' defences in World War Two.

In the castle's shadow, the little harbour of Gorey is used mainly by fishing and pleasure boats. The port was also the centre of the island's thriving oyster industry, until overfishing gradually killed it off in the 1870s. A similar boom-and-bust fate befell shipbuilding: some 120 vessels were built in Gorey between 1815 and 1879.

Other parish fortifications include towers at St. Catherine, Archirondel and Fliquet, each to the Jersey design promoted by General Conway. Victoria Tower was the last defensive round tower to be

The Esplanade

Historic Gorey harbour, dominated by the magnificent 13th-century Mont Orgueil Castle

built in Jersey, in 1837. A military barracks at Rozel is now a hotel and the Arsenal was developed as housing after the Jersey Militia's disbanding in 1946. Much older constructions, of Neolithic origin, include the Faldouet and Le Couperon dolmens.

Located in a bay on the north-eastern coast, Rozel is a tiny and picturesque port. Behind the village stands a wooded valley featuring various exotic trees planted in the 19th century. The coastal paths stretching westwards all along the island's northern coast offer splendid views and make favoured observation posts for local nature-lovers. Nearby Rozel Manor was one of the five main manor houses in the island in feudal times, though the present house was built in 1770.

Sovereignty of Les Ecréhous – a granite reef lying some six miles off this corner of Jersey – was long contested. In 1953 the court at The Hague said the reef belonged to the island and it now forms part of this parish. The reef's three islets are home to just a few 18th-century fishermen's cottages, as well as the vestiges of a medieval monastery.

The parish church, dating from the 11th century, may be the oldest centre of worship in the island. Several medieval chapels were demolished in the 19th century to make way for a horse-drawn railway, created to transport quarry stone for the building of St. Catherine's breakwater. Stretching almost half a mile out to sea, it should have been the smaller of two arms of a harbour on the east coast. The project was never completed and today the breakwater serves mainly as a platform for fishermen. Like this parish, they have much to admire out at sea.

153

Mont Orgueil Castle

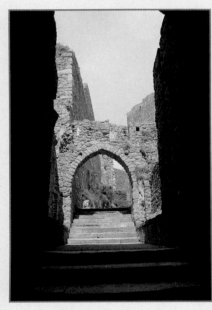

Parish of
St. MARTIN

The Red Tower at Archirondel

St. Catherine's Bay

The Ecréhous

The east coast in summer

Fliquet Bay

Parish of
St. MARTIN

The Dolmen du Couperon

The rural beauty of St. Martin's

Geoffrey's Leap

The Dolmen de Faldouet

St. Catherine's breakwater, close to half a mile long

Monument to Gorey shipbuilders

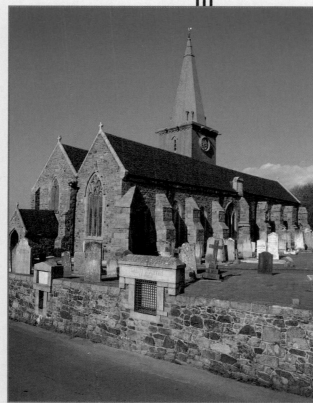
St. Martin's Parish Church

The St. Martin countryside

Highlands College, a further education establishment

Rich in Tradition

Bordering St. Helier, the relatively large parish of St. Saviour accommodates much of the overspill population of the island's capital. Though its coastline is no more than half the width of the slipway at Le Dicq, it is the location of the Rocher des Proscrits, a rock on which political refugees once fervently debated the world's ills.

The parish's best-known resident, the beautiful socialite and actress Lillie Langtry – internationally famous as the mistress of the Prince of Wales, the future Edward VII – was born in the Rectory. Although she spent much of her life abroad, 'Jersey Lily' (a pun on her name, stemming from the Pre-Raphaelite-style painting of her done by Sir John Millais, whose father was Jersey-born) is forever associated with the island. Her tomb and white marble bust are in the churchyard of the parish church, where she was twice married.

The Jersey philanthropist T.B. Davis also made his mark in St. Saviour's. He gifted Howard Davis Park to the island in 1939, in memory of his younger son killed in the First World War. The landscaped park, regarded as Jersey's most attractive, provides a quiet haven amidst the bustle of the town traffic and features a wide variety of trees and shrubs, as well as more than 60,000 colourful flowers in the summer. A statue of King George V was erected within the main entrance and a Hall of Remembrance established in the grounds. The park includes the only Commonwealth War Graves Cemetery still permitted to use wooden crosses.

The parish has the largest commercial trading estate in the island, at Rue des Prés, and a number of other commercial and light industrial businesses are in the Five Oaks area. Despite this development, the northern and eastern areas are still rural and mainly given over to agriculture. Many cattle farmers find good pasture on the higher land, while glasshouse cultivation is much in evidence, particularly at Maufant.

Government House has been the official residence

The Howard Davis Park, an oasis of calm

of all the island's Lieutenant-Governors since 1823. Close by lies the parish church, one of the largest and most beautifully situated of the island churches. It began life in the 11th century as four separate chapels, with the central tower added around 1500.

The parish's borders contain 16 schools, representing nearly two thirds of all those in Jersey, both primary and secondary. Highlands College, across the valley to the south of the church, now serves as the island's further education college. Notable buildings include the Victoria Cottage Homes almshouses, erected at Five Oaks to commemorate Queen Victoria's Diamond Jubilee and opened in 1905, and St. Saviour's Hospital, in the east of the parish. One of the island's oldest properties is Ponterrin Farm, in the Maufant area. Built around 1500, it displays fine examples of Jersey granite work. Another much-admired building is Longueville Manor, these days a luxury hotel.

One of the island's most popular museums is based in an annex of the Hôtel de France. Jersey Photographic Museum houses an impressive collection of equipment, both ancient and modern, and regularly organises exhibitions. As good a reason as any to visit this historically fascinating parish.

George V's statue in Howard Davis Park

War Cemetery, graves are marked with a simple wooden cross

Parish of
ST. SAVIOUR

Well-known Jersey residents!

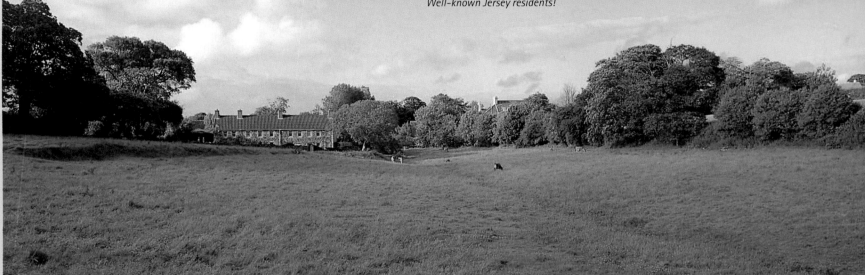

Rural St. Saviour's

Traditional Jersey farm

St. Saviour's parish hall

St. Saviour's only section of coastline, at Le Dicq slipway

The Great Hall at Highlands College

The Aquadome

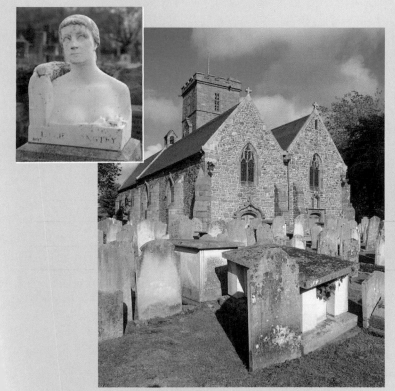
The 12th-century parish church, lasting resting place of the legendary Lillie Langtry

Le Rocher des Proscrits, meeting place of Victor Hugo and other political refugees

LE ROCHER DES PROSCRITS

VICTOR HUGO
EN EXIL
1852-1855

Royal Jersey Golf Club and Fort Henry

A proud heritage

Situated on the island's south-eastern flank, Grouville is one of only two parishes not named after a saint, the other one being Trinity. Agriculture still plays an important role here, with many farms focused on mixed farming, especially the growing of tomatoes.

Dominating the parish's natural features is the east-facing Bay of Grouville, a stretch of sand several miles long that begins at La Rocque Point and extends northwards to Gorey Harbour (which is actually in St. Martin's). Queen Victoria appreciated this bay very much and, after a visit to Jersey in 1859, she commanded her subjects to preface its name with the word 'Royal'. Today it is popular with swimmers and windsurfers, not to mention numerous wading birds in the winter.

Just behind the bay is Grouville Common. It attracts many walkers, especially in late summer when the heather is in flower. Islanders' fear of attacks by the French – following the short-lived invasion in 1781 that started at La Rocque Point and culminated in the Battle of Jersey – led to the construction of a number of defensive towers on the common in the late 18th century. While it later accommodated horse races, the area is now best known for hosting the distinguished Royal Jersey Golf Club. One of many successful golfers from the Royal was Harry Vardon. Born within putting distance of a memorial stone on the 12th fairway and commemorated by a statue at the course's entrance, he achieved six British Open victories.

At the top of the bay lies Gorey Village, a mix of original cottages and newer housing, built to complement the traditional style of island dwellings. The popular Jersey Pottery is located at its heart. To the west of the village is Queen's Valley, dammed and flooded in the 1990s to create a new reservoir for Jersey. The decision to flood this picturesque valley was controversial but, in addition to ensuring the water supply, it now provides a scenic walk for the public. Nearby Le Manoir des Prés, some eight centuries old, occasionally opens its grounds to the public. The parish church, which was first recorded in 1035, is located half a mile due south of here.

This parish also includes the Minquiers reef, which lies 12 miles (19 km) to the south of Jersey. At low tide the exposed parts of the rocky reef make Grouville the largest of the parishes, although at high tide only a few islets remain, including Maîtresse Ile. Several old fishermen's huts occupy the reef, once coveted by the French government

Golfer Harry Vardon, six-times British Open champion

Parish of
Grouville

162

La Rocque harbour

before sovereignty over it was finally awarded to the British government in 1953 by the International Court of Justice. Fishing, including oyster fishing, has always been an important industry in the surrounding seas.

Jersey's most impressive prehistoric site is La Hougue Bie, on the parish's far western side. Some three or four millennia old, the high burial mound contains a passage grave. Two tiny Medieval chapels stand on the summit. The site also includes an archaeology and geology museum, a German bunker, as well as a memorial to the slave-workers of the German occupation from 1940 to 1945. For history has clearly played an important role in shaping this parish and its community.

The Grouville countryside

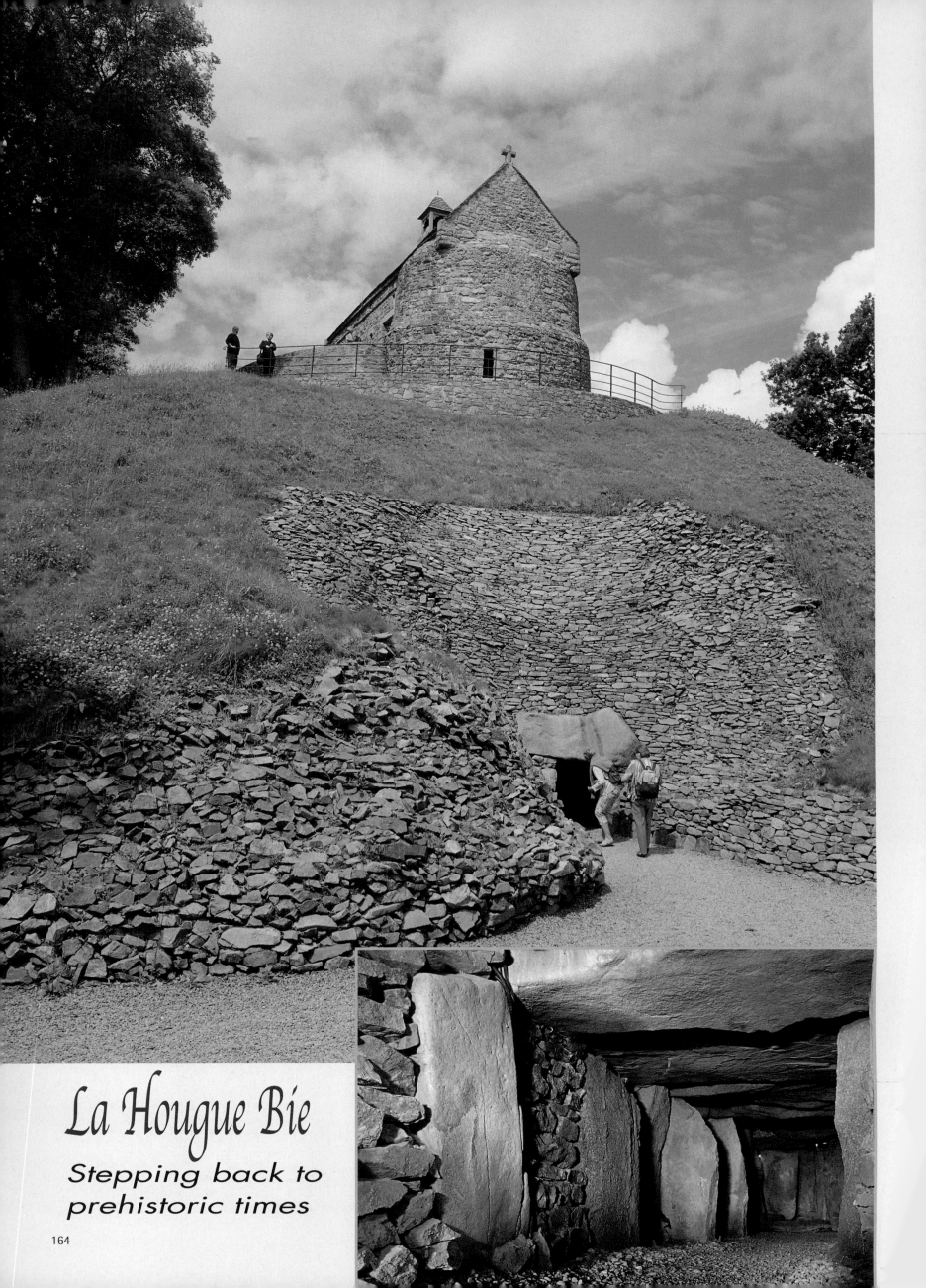

La Hougue Bie

Stepping back to prehistoric times

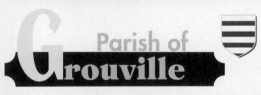

Parish of
Grouville

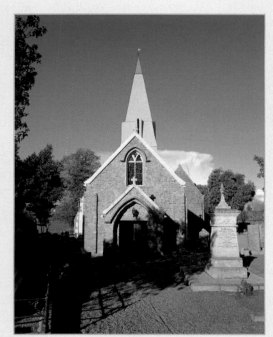

Grouville Parish Church

Les Prés Manor

Barbecue time

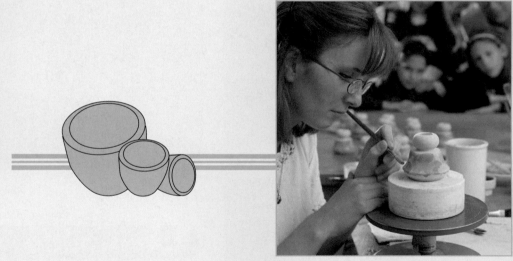

Skilled artist at the Jersey Pottery

Grouville fete

Jersey Pottery

Royal Bay of Grouville

Water-skiing in Royal Bay

The Jersey Pottery garden

Cattle country

Parish of
Grouville

Le Hocq Point, on St. Clement's Bay

Parish of St. Clement

Though it is physically the smallest of Jersey's twelve parishes, St. Clement accommodates nearly a tenth of its population. It lies on Jersey's south-east corner and includes the island's most southerly coast.

Victor Hugo, the famous French author, spent his first three years of exile in the parish. From 1852 to 1855, the great man lived at Marine Terrace, a house overlooking the sea. An active writer during his stay in Jersey, he also regularly met up with other foreign exiles living on the island.

Mainly low-lying, the parish features a marshy area known as Les Marais. At low tide a considerable expanse of beach is uncovered and the tide recedes to expose a very rocky coastline sometimes likened to a lunar landscape. Much of the coastline has sandy bays, from Grève d'Azette in the west to beyond Pontac in St. Clement's Bay. Marking the most southerly part of Jersey is Green Island, lying just yards from the sandy shore and popular with visitors. Archaeologists exploring the small grassy islet unearthed a number of box-shaped burial chambers,

Green Island

Jersey's smallest parish

in 1929 and the track has since been lost to development, although parts can still be identified and a number of the railway station buildings survive as residential accommodation.

Dating from the 11th century, the parish church is situated in the centre of St. Clement's. It stands alongside Caldwell Hall, formerly used as the parish hall before the building of a new one in 1971 at Le Hocq.

The Manor of Samarès, which has a crypt of Norman origins, is one of the island's most popular tourist destinations. Its extensive landscaped gardens, created three centuries ago, were lovingly restored and improved in the early 20th century. Attractions now include a herb garden, craft centre and a menagerie of farm animals. Just to the east of this stately home stands the Mont Ubé dolmen, estimated to be some 2,800 years old.

Considerable housing development has taken place in the parish in recent years, particularly along the coast road and in the Samarès and Les Marais areas. Grève d'Azette is home to the Florence Boot Cottages Housing Trust, one of whose original aims was to 'construct houses and cottages for the British working class', established in the 1920s by Lady Trent. Her husband founded Boots the Chemists, now a household name in the UK. Alongside are the FB Playing Fields, also donated by the Boot family, and used for many sporting events.

In the northern part of the parish, the low-lying land and south-facing slopes have produced excellent crops over the years – particularly Jersey tomatoes, which were grown both indoors and outdoors. A number of horticultural growers still make a good living from market gardening and glasshouse cultivation.

A Jersey tower at Le Hocq

possibly from the early Bronze Age period, together with other remains from even earlier periods.

The whole of Jersey's south-east intertidal region is designated a 'Ramsar' site – an internationally recognised wetland region. This ecologically important area extends from La Collette through St. Clement up to Gorey Harbour in the parish of Grouville. It includes the Violet Bank, where, on a good spring tide, more than 12 square miles of rocky shore are exposed.

The Jersey Eastern Railway Company operated train services from St. Helier to Gorey through St. Clement. The last train trundled through the parish

Le Nez Point, looking towards St. Clement's Bay

Dolmen du Mont Ubé

Low tide

Parish of St. Clement

The beach at Grève d'Azette

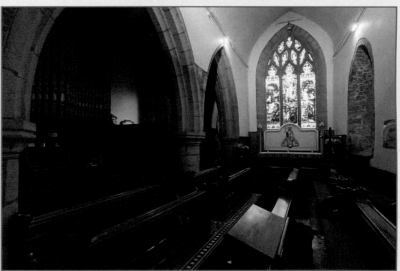
The 11th-century parish church

Falconer Richard Ellis

The Herb Garden

Samarès Manor

The Norman Colombier

The manor's magnificent dining room

The crypt, dating back to Norman times

Young falconer

Samarès Manor

Historic Victoria College

A positive teacher-student relationship

Computer skills are essential in the modern world

Education

Ensuring academic excellence

With a budget of over £74 million, Jersey's investment in all aspects of educational provision is very high – almost twice the UK's pro rata level. In recent years the island authorities have spent over £108 million pounds on remodelling and rebuilding schools. Thanks to £10 million invested in information and communication technology, students now also enjoy worldwide learning opportunities through a 'safe' wide area network.

Accommodating some 13,000 pupils, the island's schools and colleges attract good teachers and have exemplary teacher to pupil ratios. Jersey students outperform their UK counterparts in all public examinations, with 90% remaining in full-time education beyond the age of 16 and half of 18 year-olds going on to higher education.

Education in Jersey offers parents a choice of provision and a diverse range of opportunity. In primary education there are 23 non-fee-paying local States primary schools which offer places to all children aged 5 to 11. Additionally there are two single-sex States fee-paying 'prep' schools and four private primary schools. The majority of States primary schools also offer nursery classes from the age of three.

In secondary education, four non-fee-paying schools for 11 to 16 year-olds are located around the island. An additional non-fee-paying school, Hautlieu, provides for more academically able pupils, who transfer there at age 14 or 16. There are also two States single-sex fee-paying schools, Victoria College for boys and Jersey College for Girls, which cater for pupils aged 11 to 18.

The curriculum in all Jersey's secondary schools is similar to that in the UK. At key stage four, just as in the UK, students work towards GCSE examinations and in schools with sixth forms, AS and A2 level examinations.

Private secondary schools include St. Michael's, which provides for students up to the age of 14, Black's Academy, and De La Salle College and Beaulieu Convent, both single-sex Catholic schools for children from 11 to 18.

The local Careers Service offers scheduled lunchtime 'drop-in' advice at the main library each week. Every secondary school has a designated careers teacher and all students benefit from at least three weeks of work experience during their final two years of compulsory schooling. Beyond age 16, students may also learn more of the world of work and commerce through voluntary schemes such as the Institute of Directors' Work Shadowing Scheme and Young Enterprise initiatives.

Although Jersey has no university, there is a close liaison between the Island Education Service and UK universities through the Channel Islands Universities Consortium.

Jersey's Education Service works in partnership with a wide range of organisations, to ensure that everyone is able to fulfil their potential. The island is increasingly focused on lifelong learning, in order to ensure that its people remain competitive and up-to-date, and that its businesses maximise their intellectual capital.

A smile says it all

Studying in the Victoria College library

The pottery class

Ability, creativity and motivation are vital requirements for success in an island without raw material or heavy industry; 'education' is the key to unlocking and developing these skills and attitudes. The Jersey community has recognised the importance of learning and works hard to ensure that its education service is among the leaders in terms of innovation, energy, investment and outcomes.

Further education

Jersey has a very advanced economy, with the majority of its wealth created by the brains of its citizens. This 'knowledge economy' is funded by an education system that produces excellent results and sends over half of its school-leavers to universities in the UK.

Situated in St. Saviour parish and overlooking the town of St. Helier, Highlands College, a further education establishment, was opened in 1973 in a former Jesuit seminary. It offers a wide range of opportunities for full-time students and is the largest sixth-form centre in the island, providing vocational education for nearly 600 young people. Adults enrolled in the College may study up to degree and postgraduate level through various part-time courses. Its broad range of work covers construction, engineering, IT, business and secretarial studies, art and design, care and early years, leisure and tourism catering, hairdressing and beauty therapy, and media studies. The students study for a wide range of examinations, including NVQs and GNVQs, City and Guilds, the new Advanced Vocational qualifications and various profession qualifications.

Highlands is a partner college of Plymouth University and has links with several other UK universities, including Southampton, Bournemouth and South Bank. The College offers a full-time Social Science degree and part-time degrees in art, construction management and education. Masters degrees in corporate governance and education are also available.

Adult and community education is a major feature of what the college offers. The adult education provision enrols nearly 6,000 annually and classes are diverse, with everything from flower arranging to the ancient language of Jerriais taught in some 25 centres across the island. The service provides classes in English to Jersey's Portuguese community, as well as a wide range of provision for people with various learning difficulties and special educational needs.

Highlands has two distinct facilities where training is aimed at the business community. The Jersey Business School provides management training and specialist courses in finance and trust

The Jersey Business School on the Highlands College campus

A first-class education is available to all

work for the island's thriving finance industry. The School has its own Certificate in Offshore Administration and works closely with a number of professional bodies, including the Society of Trust and Estate Practitioners.

Jersey Computer Training provides the training for information technology, one of the island's emerging industries. It concentrates on technical and network training. It also offers the popular seven-module course known as the European Computer Driving Licence – a typical example of Jersey's far-sighted approach to education.

Quality education, the key to success

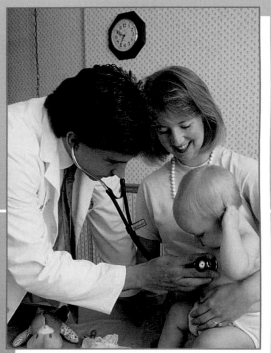

HEALTH CARE

Around a quarter of all the Jersey government's spending, some £91 million a year, goes on public health care. That works out at almost £1,040 per capita, nearly 20% more than the UK spends per head of population.

The island therefore enjoys a comprehensive health service, one which compares favourably with the UK's National Health Service and where waiting lists are generally much shorter. Nevertheless, like the NHS, Jersey's health service faces the problems of ever-increasing demand but limited resources.

The relative isolation of the island makes matters more complicated. Local hospitals and health care

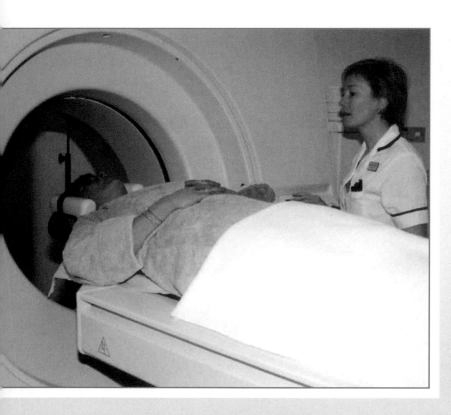

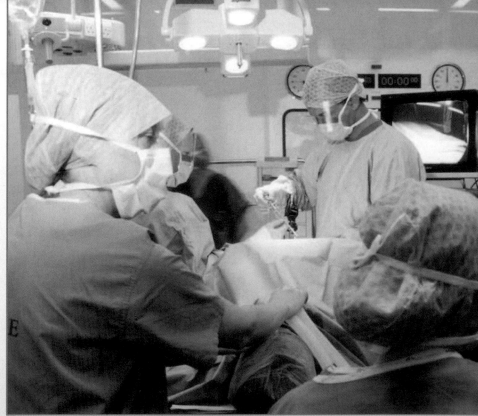

facilities have to cater for a wide range of health problems which – because of the size of the population – only affect a relatively small number of people. Few communities in Europe with a population of some 87,000 would have a general hospital offering everything from renal dialysis to in-vitro fertilisation.

However, it is impossible for Jersey, or any other community, to offer a complete range of health services – particularly as medical advances result in treatments which can be very costly. More local patients are therefore being treated in UK hospitals, under a reciprocal health agreement. This trend is likely to continue, in line with the growth in medical specialisation. Thus one of the biggest questions facing Jersey's health authorities is what services should be available locally and which could be better provided outside of the island.

Cost is only one of the factors which need to be considered when answering this question. Another is the potentially traumatic effect on patients, and their families, of having to leave the island to undergo treatment. That is one of the reasons why Jersey has invested in highly specialised equipment, such as an MRI (magnetic resonance imager) scanner, which would not normally be available in a small community. Although this

sophisticated machine is not truly cost-effective, there was considerable public support for it and local charities stepped in to help fund it. This illustrates another feature of Jersey's health care: if the government cannot afford something, charities or one of the many wealthy residents will often help out.

As in many other countries, Jersey's population is ageing, which places increasing pressure on the island's health care services. Figures from the recent census show that 40% of residents over 65 have a limiting long-term illness, and it is estimated that the number of people aged over 65 will have increased by 13% in the decade leading up to 2007. The situation is made worse by the attempt to curb immigration, which not only speeds up the demographic changes taking place but also makes it more difficult to get trained staff to help care for the ageing population.

These are some of the disadvantages of living in an island from a health care point of view. Yet there are advantages too. Jersey's small size means that it is relatively easy to coordinate all of the population's health and welfare needs and to provide 'seamless' care. Moreover, the island's size contributes to a caring attitude and there is an enormous range of charities and welfare groups available to support the health authorities.

Jersey's health care is funded differently from the UK's NHS. General practitioners are not employed by the government and patients have to pay for visits to the doctor. But the States of Jersey heavily subsidise the cost of these visits, while prescription charges of around £1.85 per item remain only a fraction of those on the mainland. Anyone on a low income can obtain medical services and prescriptions free of charge, and hospital services are free for every resident.

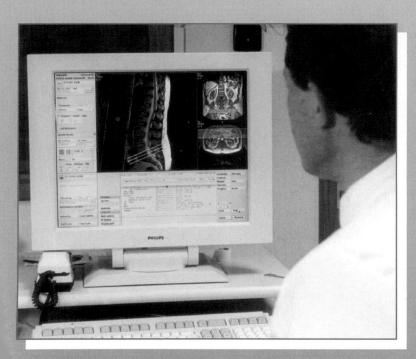

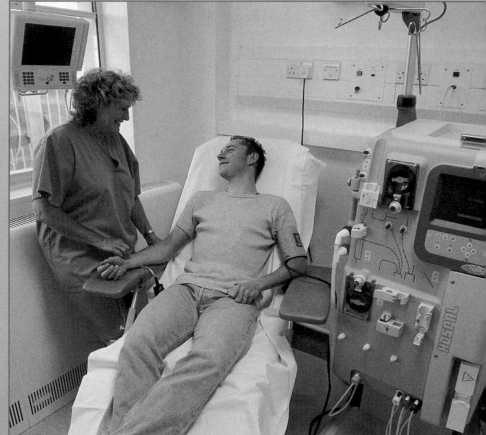

CHARACTER BUILDING

ESiC Specialist Events is a unique corporate event and training agency specialising in motivational team development, core skills training, corporate hospitality, conferences and incentives, and is also a destination management agency in Jersey. Its reputation is built on high performance and delivery of quality programmes that continually push the boundaries of creativity.

The company offers a creative, bespoke service and always gears every event or programme to the exact needs of the client in a professional and vibrant way. All team members talk from a background of credibility and are fully certified to carry out any activity themselves – everything from abseiling to flying.

Sark at speed

Windsurfing

Abseiling on Jersey's north coast

Bull's-eye!

177

St. Helier Waterfront
A world-class development

Waterfront development looking towards the Elizabeth Marina

The Waterfront, St. Helier's prestigious and comprehensive new development, represents one of Jersey's most exciting projects in years. It stretches from Les Jardins de la Mer in the west of the town to Havre des Pas in the east, and is shaping up to become a major asset for the island's marine, leisure and tourism industries.

The multi-million pound project will take some years to complete. Yet good progress has already been made, thanks to the construction of badly needed new homes and exciting leisure buildings. Recently installed or upgraded infrastructure – everything from roads to sewers and services – paves the way for further development. The growing site will also host the first new hotel to be built in the island for three decades.

St. Helier Waterfront encompasses a variety of different sites, among them promenades, gardens, harbours and piers. This reclaimed land was once a refuse tip. The turnaround is remarkable, with

Albert Pier housing development

each new completed project adding considerable value to the area as a whole.

Developed on behalf of the States of Jersey in accordance with an approved plan, the site is overseen by the Waterfront Enterprise Board. The limited company was set up in 1996 and is responsible for coordinating and promoting the town's waterfront area, including the reclamation site west of the Albert Pier as well as the Island Site, Weighbridge area and the Esplanade car park.

The Victorian Havre des Pas pool

Topping up the tan

Maritime House, home to the port authority administration offices

Relaxing at Les Jardins de la Mer

This project is certainly ambitious. It will meet some of the current and future needs of Jersey's economy, and in particular will be a boom to its tourism industry. It will also open up the waterfront to the public and create an attractive green environment. Careful planning and monitoring ensure that all development is balanced and sustainable, and well integrated with St. Helier.

Completed projects already include Maritime House, Elizabeth Marina, Waterfront Car Park plus two major public parks and promenades. Housing for rent and for purchase by first-time buyers is also springing up at Albert Pier.

On the leisure side, there is a new complex known simply as the Waterfront. This is the first major privately funded development of its kind in Jersey, also supported by the public sector. The complex comprises a water park, featuring a range of pools and rides, and commercial leisure facilities that include a ten-screen cinema, nightclub, pub and themed cafe, as well as a state-of-the-art health and fitness centre. Nationally renowned operators will run all these facilities.

Les Jardins de la Mer proudly claim to offer something for everyone – not least the maritime woodland, a rockery, shingle beds and lawns. The traditionally designed gardens contain a unique circular maze, made up of hedges and water jets that rise and fall intermittently. Few people reach the maze's central statue without getting soaked in the process... but on a hot summer's day, nobody really minds! Smaller year-round attractions include go-karts, trampolines, sand sculpture and a skateboard park. La Frégate, a striking beach cafe located within the gardens, is the work of the respected architect Will Alsop. Resembling an upturned wooden boat, it has become a popular venue for local events.

Visitors and residents tempted by the great outdoors can stroll along the resplendent new promenades, some leading to the two other new gardens situated around the area. Yet not everything here is fresh off a draughtsman's board. The bathing pool at Havre des Pas first opened in 1895, serving as a swimming pool for locals and a leading tourist attraction. The spirit and atmosphere of this charming Victorian lido have been retained, thanks to delicate restoration, coupled with some necessary modernisation.

Maritime House, erected adjacent to Albert Pier and the St. Helier Marina, is home to the island's harbour, immigration and customs authorities. The attractive three-storey building stands on one of several sites in the area set aside for the States' own accommodation requirements.

A number of other new projects have been completed, including La Collette Boat Hoist and Quay and Ariadne, the world's largest steam clock. Found at the top of the New North Quay and powered by a genuine steam engine, the specially commissioned clock is shaped like a paddle steamer – once so familiar a sight in the local harbour. It also helps to attract visitors to the nearby award-winning Maritime Museum.

The jewel in the crown among the new developments will be the Waterfront Hotel, located alongside Elizabeth Marina. Part of an international hotel chain, this 230-room establishment will offer the level of quality and service expected by today's sophisticated tourist and business visitors. The hotel will feature a range of suites, as well as at least two first-class restaurants, a brasserie, conference/banqueting facilities and business centre. Once complete, this hotel will likely represent the island's largest ever private-sector investment in tourism.

Housing has not been left out of the equation. Jersey urgently needs new homes and the Waterfront will make a significant contribution in this field. Most of the new homes will be offered for purchase to locally qualified residents. Albert Pier has some rented accommodation too, some of it intended for the disabled. The modern and innovative apartments here, numbering around 150, were designed by local architects and benefit from their own underground car parking plus private balconies looking out over the busy harbour. More private-sector housing is planned, including mixed housing and commercial schemes for the redeveloped Esplanade car park site.

Much work still remains to be done under this important project. There are plans for several 'icon' buildings, possibly a botanic garden and a national art gallery, not to mention a feature footbridge linking the town centre to this site. An events area, modern transportation centre and offices are also expected to make an appearance. However, the Waterfront Enterprise Board already takes heart from the evident success of existing infrastructure and buildings, which have injected vitality and a great sense of optimism into the island's leisure and tourism sectors.

Watermaze at Les Jardins de la Mer

Index

Jersey Organisations and Government Departments

Jersey Financial Services Commission, tel.: +44 (0)1534 822000, www.jerseyfsc.org • Jersey Heritage Trust, tel.: +44 (0)1534 633300, www.jerseyheritagetrust.org • Jersey Finance Ltd., Tel.: +44 (0)1534 836000, www.jerseyfinance.je • Jersey Tourism, tel.: +44 (0)1534 500700, www.jersey.com • Environmental Services, tel.: +44 (0)1534 601458, www.env.gov.je • Harbours, tel.: +44 (0)1534 885588, www.jersey-harbours.com • Sports and Recreation, tel.: +44 (0)1534 500200, www.slr-online.com • Agriculture and Fisheries, tel.: +44 (0)1534 866200, www.agfish.co.uk • Business Names and Companies Registry, tel.: +44 (0)1534 822030, www.jerseyfsc.org